The Adventures of "Woody" Walker,
Attorney, Farmer, WWII Soldier

by Woodrow Walker

RoseDog Books
PITTSBURGH, PENNSYLVANIA 15222

ISBN: 978-1-4349-9362-5
Printed in the United States of America

First Printing

For more information or to order additional books,
please contact:
RoseDog Books
701 Smithfield Street
Pittsburgh, Pennsylvania 15222
U.S.A.
1-800-834-1803
www.rosedogbookstore.com

To the memory of
my Mother and Father.

Contents

Acknowledgments

First, I would like to thank my friend Marvel Rasmussen (now Zona), whose friendship with me goes back to high school, for suggesting this autobiography; she says mine is an interesting life. She also has nominated me as an outstanding graduate of Greenville High School.

Also, Laura Jackson, court reporter, for coaching, for supervising the typing and editing from the original, yellow legal-pad, handwritten copy.

Also, the Dorance Publishing Company for their suggestions and editing of this book.

May I thank one of the women in my life whose influence has had a profound effect on this life: my mother, Mildred Walker (maiden name Chase). As my smart father, Craig Walker (he was valedictorian of his high school class while going only half days) passed when I was eight years old, she raised me and guided me especially when important issues emerged.

My sister, Elaine, another woman of my life who had great faith in my intellectual abilities and insisted that I go to college. She had me stay with her while attending the University of Detroit for two years. Otherwise, we would not have the funds to go to college during the Great Depression.

My beloved wife, Janet, another woman of my life, and the love of my life, who was my right arm during forty-one years of solo law practice. She was more than a legal secretary: she was an office manager. She also was at my side at the Front Royal Farm helping with fence repair and fence work. I retired from law practice to take care of her for four-and-a-half years. She is now in an assisted living home in Front Royal, near the farm. She has the support of the entire family.

I would like to thank Justice Oliver Wendell Holmes Jr. for a quote of his reading like this (I am not sure that it's 100% accurate but it's pretty close):

"No one has earned the right to intellectual ambition unless he has learned to dig by the diving rods for springs, which he may never reach."

I had this posted on the wall while I was going to night law school. And, for me, the writing of this book is an intellectual challenge, and with the help of many people who encouraged and assisted me through editing and just their support.

My daughter in law Kathy, made the poignant comment that the life of this one American was interwoven with the American history of that time.

Woodrow Walker
2822 Ft. Scott Drive
Arlington, Virginia

Chapter I
Ancestors

May we talk a little about my family's ancestors and their economic standing. I find them interesting. According to my niece, Martha Weldon (she had done a study of this matter), the Walkers go back to the 1600s and migrated to Canada in the late 1700s. My Grandmother Walker, whose maiden name was Watson, came to this country from England during the Civil War. My cousin, Virginia Walker (whose maiden name is now Wood) was down on our farm, reading from Grandmother Walker's diary. I will share more later.

Grandmother Walker wrote that two of her brothers were in the Union Army during the Civil War. One of her brothers was killed at the Battle of Perryville. The other brother contracted tuberculosis and died from it. She wrote, "Here were two English boys that got involved in a fight that was not their fight."

My understanding was that she found it hard to adjust to this country because it was so rough as compared to the refined living of England. She talked about Indians going by her window. They were friendly Indians.

She married William Walker, who was 20 years older than her. William Walker, my grandfather, had a saw mill in Greenville, my hometown. There is a picture of the mill in the Greenville museum. He was also a pharmacist in Trufant, Michigan. Henry Meijer has his barber's chair in the Museum. She read to us from Grandmother Walker's diary, in a finished room in the barn, which was built by my son Bill. Of course Grandfather Walker died first, leaving her with five children. My father, Craig Walker was sent to his Aunt Kate's farm in Gratiot County, Michigan. My father, of course, worked on the farm.

My father came to Greenville to attend high school. He paid board to Grandmother Walker, because she needed the money. He worked in the bookstore one half of the day and went to high school the other half. He graduated valedictorian of his high school class after attending only half days. He was a smart man.

Craig Walker's handwriting was just plain beautiful. He used the old time penmanship. He later became town clerk, working nights to pay off a debt of his brother Will Walker. He later went into a partnership with my uncle Will Chase in the potato and coal business. At this time, Michigan was one of the leading, if not *the* leading, state in producing potatoes.

My niece Martha stated that in Canada, a Chase married a French girl. Hence, I have a small amount of French blood of which I never knew. My great grandmother Davidson was Irish and lived to be ninety-eight, according to my mother. She would get up at 5:00 A.M. to work in the garden. The doctor said that her parts just wore out, meaning her body wore out.

At this time—the end of World War I—the partnership had warehouses throughout the state of Michigan. The warehouses were full to the brim of potatoes and the price was at the unheard rate of five dollars per bushel. My dad said, "Sell," and Will Chase said, "Hold." Do I need to tell you what happened? Of course, the bottom dropped out of the market. My mother said my father came home at ten in the morning and went to bed. He was literally sick.

Both of my grandfathers died before I was born. Grandfather Chase apparently owned or had control of, vast amounts of timberland around Lakeview, Michigan.

Now, I do not know what the facts are regarding the failure of his timber business. Timber was the way he made his living. He lost all of it in the panic of the 1890s. I do not know if he had options to buy or owned the timberland. The fact is, he lost all of it. He went into a depression.

In hand-me-down statements, some said he lost it because he could not pay the taxes. I also heard he lost it to Sharpsters from Grand Rapids, Michigan. My dad, Craig Walker, said what he could have done with the timber. His grandson, yours truly, along with his wife, Janet, own timber in Front Royal, Warren County, Virginia. 108 acres of fine hardwoods, including black walnuts. We sold four lots or acreage off (eleven acres) in 2003. The farm and all land is paid for, and their titles insured by Chicago Title. I will tell you later about this beautiful farm.

In 2008, we sold the black walnuts. The logger said it was the best black walnuts he had seen outside of those that grew on limestone. (See the picture of my grandson standing on some of the black walnut logs.) Bill and Jon have planted ninety-five black walnuts—two seedlings to a stump—this year. We have given back to the land.

Chapter II

Early Childhood

I remember when I was three years old, spending a great deal of time in Mr. McIntire's wood-working shop with lots of wood ships. Apparently I had been taken to a movie involving Jack Holt and a tiger. He would kid with me about Jack Holt and the tiger. That is the about the only recollection I have of very early childhood at the Montcalm Street house.

After living at the Montcalm Street house, my parents moved to the Thompson house on North Lafayette Street. This house had five acres, a barn, a chicken house, a pig house, and an extra lot. My father always wanted a farm. This is the closest he ever got to it. Nowadays, this property would be considered a mini farm. I am sure he would have obtained a farm if he had lived longer. The Thompson house was large, with a large living room, dining room, kitchen, downstairs pantry, and a basement with a place for fruit and vegetables as well as four bedrooms and one upstairs bathroom. It also had a large, screened-in front porch and a backyard. It was a house fitting for a family of six and Grandmother Chase, who had come to live with the family in her last days.

I remember being fascinated by the sitting hens with their little chicks. There was a hog house in the back of the barn. Early childhood was spent here, and kindergarten at the Pearl Street Elementary School.

In the back of the barn between the hog house and the chicken house was the Darby gravel pit, off to the side of my parents' property. At the bottom

4

was water. We called it a pond. (In law, this attraction for boys today would be called "an attractive nuisance." In my service at American Law as an attorney I did a research of federal cases on the "Attractive Nuisance Doctrine.")

Another neighbor's child and I, both of us under five, were down at the bottom of the gravel pit. Mr. Darby had a long, white, flowing beard. He came out yelling at us. We were scared right out of our pants. We tried running up the side of the gravel pit. With the loose gravel, it seemed like we were running in place with our little legs. You get the picture. However, somehow we beat him. I headed for home.

Toward the supper hour, Mr. Darby came up on the front porch and looked in the window. He could see me and Grandmother Chase. Grandmother asked, "Isn't there somebody at the door?"

I responded, "No, Grandmother, there is nobody at the door." He came several times with the same result.

Mr. Darby must have gotten in touch with my parents later because in my stocking at Christmastime was a note that said, "Do not go into the Darby gravel pit, from Santa Claus." Of course, later on, we did. We also put fish in the pond from Flat River.

Another incident of early childhood took place at my father's potato office. This incident was such a close call with death that I may not have lived to tell you about it now. I had gotten a new tricycle—my pride and joy. My mother had left me at the office while she did some shopping. There was a bench across from the office on Lafayette Street. Under the direction of men on the bench across the street, I crossed over to the office. So far so good. After I went back, the men said it was all clear to cross the street. Now, at this time (the early 1920s), there was not much traffic in a town of about four thousand. I started back. A lady in a speeding car came up fast. Instead of staying in her lane, she crossed over to the other lane. If she would have stayed in her lane she would have missed me. She hit me and the tricycle. I was thrown up in the air and landed on the pavement on my head. I lay unconscious.

When my Dad came out to take me to Dr. Weaver, he could not step on the starter. Someone else had to drive. The driver was the bookkeeper. The driver carried me upstairs to Dr. Weaver's office, which was over near Wycoff's Shoe Store. My mother was coming down the stairs as her limp little boy was being carried upstairs. She went into Wycoff's Shoe Store. Mr. Wycoff put her under a fan. Mr. Wycoff asked, "What's the matter, Mrs. Walker?" She could only point upstairs.

Dr. Weaver instructed my parents to take me home and, when I came, for me to ask certain questions. I answered all of the questions correctly. Dr. Weaver said that in that case I would be fine. Being a parent myself during these times, I can understand the anguish they must have endured that day. Additionally, my brother Ralph was so upset he closeted himself in the hayloft and would not come out for supper.

In February, my parents enrolled me at the age of five in kindergarten at the Pearl Street School. Thus, I was in half-year classes straight through to high school and graduation. My mother was the president of the Parents Teachers Association. It was a bigger job than it sounds. I figured that out later on in life.

Later on in school, a certain neighborhood boy got me to skip school. My father spent all afternoon looking for me. I will say, it was the one time I was disciplined. I was, shall we say, "taken to the woodshed." My mother later said she was going to intervene.

The parents of both of us got together. I was not to associate with this boy. I abided by parents' decision. Later, the boy went to reform school. My parents were ahead of their time in handling juveniles and keeping them on the right path. In my law practice, in adult life, it was my objective to keep juveniles on the right path, to follow through after the court case was over.

My father started off his married life by working at Tower's Ironworks as a bookkeeper at ten dollars per week. How he could support a wife and buy a house is beyond me. I do know that a dollar was worth a lot more back then than it is now.

Let me say that if my father had any vices, they were playing cards, drinking Coca-Cola and smoking cigarettes at the Smoke House in Greenville. I remember my mother would not allow us to eat dinner until he came home from the Smoke House.

Two of these habits caught up with him. He developed Bright's disease of the kidneys, becoming very ill. Dr. Weaver sent him to Kellogg's Sanitarium at Battle Creek, the leading sanitarium at that time. Dialysis had not been discovered. Kellogg said, "There is nothing we can do for him," sending him home to die. He was forty-two years old. He died in his new house, which he just recently finished. He was not a religious man but said he had been to the kingdom and was ready to go.

While my father was at the sanitarium, I stayed at Uncle Will's house on Washington Street. It was a stately built house. At age eight, I wrote a letter to my dad.

The Thompson House also had a large lot on which my father built "the new house," a bungalow. He did not get to enjoy the new house very long as he died in that new house, a grey-shingled bungalow.

I loved that house. Perhaps it played some part in the purchase of our first house in 1950, a grey-shingled bungalow built in 1926. We will get to that purchase later.

During my life at the Thompson House, my father and Will Chase kept two cows in the barn during the wintertime. They kept the cows in a pasture below Grandmother Chase's house on Flat River. My brother, Ralph and I used to pick up Indian arrowheads on this pasture. They also maintained two hogs in the hog house. My dad had chickens in the chicken house.

There was a large turnout at my father's funeral at Brown's Funeral Home. He was well-liked in the town. I was sad to see my mother cry so much.

MY POULTRY REVIEW'S

By Woodrow Walker, age 11

My Poultry Reviews

This story is no make my story is all about W.W. Walker Poultry Adventures when he was very young with his young playmate. It goes on with dogs eating his chicks and roosters chasing him

The beginning of my poultry business is very humble. My father was always making a little garden or fussing with an acre of corn or potatoes. It was right in my father and mothers farm. We had a big barn with two cows and two pigs. We also had a chicken coop about fifteen feet in length and about ten ft. wide. So we had a nice flock of chickens.

One day a black chicken got out and got run over: The place it got hit was in the leg. My father said that I could have her. This was the beginning of my poultry business. This poor little chicken got a ride in my little wagon each day. And this was my favorite playmate so it never got any chance to lay any eggs. Ever since that I have had a great love for poultry.

In the year of 1929 a boy named Fred and I went to get some little baby chicks. Besides this I took what little change. It amounted to about seventy five cents. We either had to go around a dam or make a short cut across the River. But how were we to get across. There were some boats there and not locked. So we took one of the boats and started acrossed. The man that owned them was a little man and poor too. He only had six little chicks to sell. One was a Rhode Island Red and the rest was Single Comb. White Leghorns. He wanted fifteen cents for one, but he knew me so he let me have them for ten cents a piece. So we started home. I kept them for about three days when the Rhode Island Red got pretty dumby and soon died. Soon three more died that left tow. They were about eight weeks old now.

The place I planned to keep my chicks was in my mothers chicken coop. When my mother built her new house she also built a new chicken coop right in back of the garage. She also bought chicks of this same man that is how I knew where to get them. But she killed them all but a great big yearling Rooster. Of course we kids teased him and made him ugly.

One day he got out of the park and of course he was always chasing us. I remember one morning when I just got up and was standing in front of the garage doors to sun myself, when all of a sudden something hit me in the legs like a bullet. I turned around and there stood that old rooster all crouched ready to spring on me if I moved an inch. Then I started to run just as fast as I could for the front yard with him right after me. But we soon ate him and that was the last of him.

These were the only two chickens I had just then. They were always gone in the day but came at night.

I had a hound pup named Sport and one day I got up and Sport had just killed them. He didn't kill them because he was hungry because of the sport.

Now I didn't have any chicks at all. Some people told me that a man named Blanding had some white leghorn chicks for 10¢ a piece.

Boy I sure thought this was some bargain. I had one dollar in my draw with which to buy my chicks. My mother said that I could not go so far. But I was determined to go. So a great friend of mine named George Gould said that he knew the way out and another little friend named Billy Richmond also went. There was nobody in the United States better friends at that time.

So we started out about 9 o'clock in the morning. We had to cross fields and woods to reach there. When we finally did reach there we asked the man if he would sell some of his chicks. He said that you had to order them ahead of time before you could get any. So we started homeward. When we got part way home I reached in my pocket for my dollar and it was gone. Just then the 11:30 whistle blew. George and Billy should have been home by this time. So they started home just as fast as they could while I went back to hunt for my dollar. But it was no place to be found. So I went home very down hearted. I thought that was what I got for not minding my mother.

One morning in about July I thought I would go out to Blandings, because I had ordered them ahead of time. This time I took a road that led to across Flat river. But this wasn't where the boats were.

I was walking barefooted on the gravel and it didn't feel too nice. First I tried walking on the grass but the ditches were too big and I couldn't make any progress. But I finally did reach Blandings and you ought to see those then little white balls. I raised them until they were about three weeks old. One day I was playing out in back of my house in a pond. George and I put a bunch of fish down there and they hatched about ten times as many. We had some little rafts too. We were playing along when George's dad came along he thought sure that he was going to get a licken. But his dad said that we kids could go fishing. When I went to look at my chicks Sport had got into the park and killed them.

All I had left now was two pullets and one rooster. I was thinking the next day about getting some old hens, but not any chicks. I called up Blanding for some, but he said that he couldn't spare any. He said that his brother had some Wyandotts. His brother said that he would sell me three old hens. That afternoon I drew $4.00 out of my school saving's account. When I got home he had three old hens and two pullets, I asked him why he brought the pullets over. He said that mother said to bring them over. He said it amounted to nearly five dollars. I had only drew out four dollars out. He said that he would trust me on the other dollar. One day I saw him in a store told him to come on over and I would pay him. But he never showed up. I have kept those chickens until just lately.

I couldn't stand it any longer I just had to have some more chickens. So one night me and a boy named Stan planned it over that night which was Saturday. Stan said he could get a couple of burlap bags. The place I was going to get the chickens was Roy Brinks. When we started I don't believe that we knew where we were going. When we had walked about a half of mile it seemed like ten miles. We asked a lot of people where Roy Brinks was some of them knew and some of them didn't. The chickens that Mr. Brink had for us were nice Wyandott pullets. They amounted to almost $1.00 a piece. We bought five of them. Stan carried three and I carried two. Let me tell you it seemed a long time before we reached home.

One day George and I and a few other boys were playing fox and geese. Our neighbor Mrs. McMillan went South for her health and took her daughter Myrtie Schenfield with her. While her other daughter Gertie from the farm came down to stay in her house.

In the back of her car were five white leghorn pullets. I asked her how much she wanted for them. She said that she wanted five dollars for them so this deal was made. But I couldn't get them that day because it was Sunday. The next morning I found some sparrows eating my grain. I thought I would set a trap for them that noon. So when I got home with my money George Edgecomb came with me. When we shut the doors and peeped in behold there were fifteen sparrows. George didn't take no pity on the sparrows. After we caught a few alive we went over to Gerties and got the chickens. I now had seventeen chickens.

I will have to tell you about my incubator. So our neighbors and I went out to Blanding's to see if it was alright. He said that he never had any good luck with small incubators. But he said that he knew people who did. So I sent for it the next day. Finally while the days dragged along, when one day I got a letter from the Express office. It said that there was a pakage for me. So before I did get it there was a lot of fussing around and when I did get it what do you spose it was? It was a brooder for baby chicks.

About a month after that I kept getting letters to buy some baby chicks. Of course I got all excited and one day I sent away to the Superior hatchery Windsor Missouri for twenty five chicks. Of course I had to have something to keep them warn in. So I sent away for this same brooder. Then I ordered fifty more chicks of ". One day a box of baby chicks arrived and I looked in and there was thirty baby chicks in it. I thought these were the chicks that came from Missori because you know that (you) get a few extras because some can't stand the journey. Then who do you think drove in? It was Blanding coming with some chicks. But he came after his money. You see I bought the brooder from Montgomery Ward & Co. So you see the brooder came before the chicks from Missouri. Blanding's chicks were the ones under the brooder. When Mrs. Blanding came in I said come on down in the basement and see my chicks. So when he went down there he told us that they were his chicks. My wasn't I surprised? So I paid him just as soon as we came up stairs. He told me I shouldn't buy chicks out of state but that didn't stop me any. The reason he only brought thirty was because he was all sold out. I had ordered my chicks from Missouri the first of January but nothing (showed up) One day I got a card about the first of March, it said that my chicks would be here about March 14(1929) but the chicks never showed up until about the 21 of March. While the chicks were growing it came spring vacation. Mrs. McMillen had come back and Gertie came in to the town for groceries. She asked me if I wouldn't want to come out to her farm and stay a while. I said that I would very much. I don't believe that my Mother wanted me to go very much. The first night I was out there we played rum beat most of the time so we didn't play rum anymore nights. The next day I was out to Gerties I made me a kite and so you see I spent most of my time flying my kite. After the day of flying my kite I went over to where Mr. Eurick was that one day while he was cutting wood a green peace flew off and almost hit a man. The man that owened the buzz saw was Wayne Debree. He had some game chickens so I wanted some game chicken too. So after the vacation was over I told Wayne Debree to come to town and we will make a deal. So the next day he came to town before I tell you about my deal I will have to tell you about my Turkey. One day my brother went out into the country to get a hunting dog and I went with him. While my brother and the farmer were talking I was out with his wief watching her getting the

Turkeys to bed. She said that there was a little turkey who didn't have any brothers and sisters. You see all her brothers and sisters died. She said the next time I came out there I could have him. So when my brother took the dog back I got the Turkey. The next day all the kids in the neighborhood was playing with her. So Wayne Debree came down to make a deal with me. I said that I would give him a Turkey and one Single comb white leghorn, rooster for two game hens and one registered white leghorn hen. He gave me a game hen to keep a (with) a game rooster. But the rooster died. (Now I had twenty) one chickens all together. This was quite a bunch for a little boy like me to tend to ever morning. I get about 30 (eggs) a week not counting how much (it) costs. One day after I had my chickens for about nine months I thought I would get all my chickens and get one kind. This kind was Rhode Island Reds.

Before I sell my chickens I'll have to tell you about my Rose comb Buff Leghorns. You see I still wanted some more chickens. One day I was walking around to get some more chickens and some men told me a man named Mr. Bishop had some chickens. So I went over to his house and asked him how much he wanted for some of his chickens. He said that he got his chickens directly from Madison square and so he wanted $2.00 a pice for his high bred chickens. I thought this was to much. But he had Rose comb Buff leghorns. He said that he wanted seven dollars for six of them. He did have another one but it only had one wing. But he said that he wouldn't sell her for five dollars. He had a rooster to but he wanted four dollars for it so I wouldn't buy him.

He said he wouldn't sell them to me until I told my mother about it. So I got my Rose Comb Buff Leghorns all right.

One day I was wrapping butter down to the creamery for ice cream of course. Some of the men down there told me about a man named Mr. Miller and he had five thousand little baby chickens.

One day he came down to the creamery for some butter milk. This was in Jan.. So I went over and saw Mr. Eurick to see if he wanted any. He said that he beleied that he would go out and look around. When we got out there my what an afull sight the chicks were in. One would topple over every minute. Then he had some pullets. They were pretty good. He wanted 50¢ a piece for them. So I bought eight of them. The reason the chicks were dieing so was because he had lost patience and he didn't burn his brooder. I bought twelve of them for ten cents and Henery bought the rest for one dollar. I guess Mr. Miller wanted to get rid of his chicks afull bad. Mr. Eurick kept his chickens until just lately when I bought them and ate them.

One day I thought I would get an old setting hen and hatch some of my owen little baby chicks. A boy named Larison said that his dad had an old setting hen. He said that he wanted $1. for it. So I bought it. But it never hatched any chicks.

Then I went up to Mr. neilsens who has some Rhode Island Reds. So I bought to of them for $2. But they never hatched any either.

One day I got an egg mash feeder and a grit box. If anybody ever wants to get lots of eggs they would be wise to get them.

Now I must get back when I was going to sell my chickens. I was going to sell my chickens and get all one kind. This kind was Rhode island Reds, where I was going to get them was up to Mr. Nelsons.

So Mr. Bannen came up and got my chickens. He gave me twenty-two cents a (pound). So the next morning he came up and got my chickens. Then that noon I went up to Mr. Nelsons to get my Rhode Island Reds. He said that he believe that he wanted to sell his chickens just now because they were laying to good. Of course I wanted my other chickens back so he brought them back.

One day a man named Roy Chase was going out into the country after potatoes and he was my cousin so I went with him. When we got to our distance, We asked the people if they would sell any chickens, They told us that in the mid winter an old hen hatched three little chicks.

if the man would of had his way about it he would of killed them.

So I bought the three of them for one dollar.

So the time came when I finally did sell all my chickens but the Rose Comb Buff Leghorns and the one I got in the country.

A man named Peter Larison bought this bunch of chickens for twenty three cents a pound.

So I was going to get a lot of chicken. So if you were going to have a lot of chickens you'd have a nother chicken coop. Well let me tell you we scraped and done everything to get boards enough for the coop. Finally we did get the wood up. Now we needed Tar paper and cello glass. Then when it was all done Mother told Ralph to tear it down.

He started 9 o'clock in the morning but never got it all down until about 4 o'clock in the afternoon because there was quite an argument.

Well it came time and I wanted some more chickens. So I called up Mr. Miller for some pullets, by he had just sold out.

Mrs. McMillen said that she would take me down to Ceader springs hatchery. So we went down there Saturday. While Mrs. McMillen went into talk to the owner while I went out to decide what kind of chicks I wanted. I was going to get some little baby chicks, but Mrs. Mcmillen said if she were me she would get some 6 weeks old Barred Rocks and I believe she gave me some good advice. They cost me thirty seven cents a piece.

The next day Mrs. McMillen was fixing a pen for them. I kept them until just lately when I sold them to my Mother for $4.

My brother owed me quite a lot of money and he had a few chickens out in back which were these kind, one Rhode Island Red rooster, 3 Wyandotts and one Plymouth Rock rooster. I took the Rhode Island Red and the springer up to Ray Hart the chicken Man. But he wasn't there so I started down to the meat makets. So as I came out of the ally I noticed a sign and it said Cream, Poultry eggs. So I went in there and got 60¢ for my springer. But they would only give me 9¢ a pound for the (syag) so I wouldn't sell him. I stayed there awhile getting warm. When Mr. O'neil asked how much I would give him for 5 Baty pullets. I said that I didn't have no use for such chickens. He said that he would sell me the 5 for 35¢ a peice. I made believe that it was an afull price. But I really did think it was cheap. Finally he said he would give me 3 pullets for the rooster if I would buy the rest so this deal was made. So I started home with chickens and 10¢.

I never thought of keeping those Batys. So I knew a man named Pete and we made a deal like this. He gave me 30¢ and a Baty Rooster.

I forgot to tell you that I built another chicken coop where people from the road couldn't see it. that is why the other one was toren down. You know those little chicks I got from Missouri they were halh growen up when I sold them to Mr. McFaland for 30¢ a peice. This is the deal we made. I had bought two Ducks for two $ a peice. I gave him thease and the pullets. Then he gave me 6 Barrd Rocks and one 10# Rabbit. Then I sold it for (3$). Then I got 50¢ too. The White Leghorn roosters I sold for #2.00. While I was taking them up to market I met Billy. So Billy and I started for Roy Brinks again. We also took our dinners. Finally we reached there and we got 4 leghorn pullets for $3.00. Billy carried 1 and I carried 3. When we starred home we took cross lots across plowed fields and when we got halfway home Billy says this leave them here. Now I had $60.00 in the bank and a bunch of chickens, a chicken coop, a brooder, layer mash feeder and a grit box. The End.

Chapter III

Early Poultry and Agriculture Business

My early poultry endeavors are best described by my Poultry Reviews. Mrs. McMillan, our great next-door neighbor, drove me down to Cedar Springs to buy some six-week-old chickens. They would not die. She built an enclosed chicken pen in the back of her garage. I later built a chicken house on the back of her barn, with her permission.

I will now tell you about this remarkable Michigan woman. She had no husband at the time, but lived with one grown daughter. She was a retired rural mail delivery carrier for the U.S. Mail. She delivered the mail by sleigh in the winter time. She traded horses with this horse trader who gave her a doped up horse. The horse slumped down as she got the him home. She took him back to the trader's barn, broke off the lock, and took her old horse back. Later, she was on her route in the sleigh when the trader jumped out of the bushes and grabbed her horse by the bridle. He said, "If you were a man I would whip you." Now, Mrs. McMillan was a strapping woman of great strength. Mrs. McMillan grabbed her horse whip, turned it around in the air and said, "Do not let that stop you." End of horse trade.

I was in the chicken business until we moved to what I call "The Michigan Farm." In the summer of 1937 I raised some chickens for a chicken hatcher. He was to buy them in the fall at an agreed price. I took them down there along with my girlfriend Dorothy. As I recall, he gave me less than what I thought he should have given, and less than to what he had agreed. He said, "Take it or leave it." What could I say? We will talk about this very good farm later. Suffice to say for here that I went into a partnership with Mrs. Alvin Sharp who lived down the road. We bought two-hundred white rock chicks each. She had a brooder house, and she raised the chicks until they were six weeks old. I furnished the feed—and could they eat feed. They were really cute. This was the summer of 1938. We moved the old chicken house from 909 Lafayette Street to a field in the farm. We had raised wheat and corn at the farm. I lavishly fed the chickens with this feed; they had a full range around the chicken house—no fence. I trained them to stay off of the county gravel road. What a quality of life these chickens had as compared to present-day chickens that live in a crowded wire cage. Of course, they were much better chickens for the consumer. I sold these chickens to Mr. Nelson's Meat Market. He told me they were the best chickens he had ever had in his market.

Let me say I was quite busy as a child in agricultural pursuits. I raised potatoes, sweet corn, and tomatoes. I sold these products to the people of Greenville. My agriculture teacher and my principal Ben Dobbin were very encouraging.

I had always wanted a pony. In order to have my own, I asked my father and mother to have my uncle Tom Owen in New Mexico send one here (he owned a ranch). He stated it would cost too much for transportation to send a pony. A pony saddle and bridle went on sale for fifteen miles north of Greenville. I hitchhiked to this destination, paid for the pony out of my earnings, and rode the pony back, later buying a harness and buggy. Of course, I sold the sweet corn and potatoes from my buggy.

I had a scary incident with this pony. Another close call Her name was Jesse. She had a blind eye on the left side. I was riding her down a dirt road in North Greenville. A car went by on her blind side causing her to jump sideways, throwing me off. My foot got caught in the stirrup. I was dragged me on the dirt road toward the main paved street, Lafayette Street. In the meantime I was hollering, "Whoa, whoa!" She stopped at the paved street. I dusted myself off and got back on the saddle, none the worse for the wear.

Let me give advice to any first time (or "green") horse rider: if you get thrown off a horse get right back on that horse, or the chances are very good that you will never ride a horse again. Further, you have got to let the horse know who is the boss or the horse will be the boss. Horses are a lot smarter than a lot of people give them credit. I say this with the perspective of owning horses and a pony on the beautiful Front Royal Farm now for thirty-six years. We will talk later about this beautiful farm. This is truly God's Country. My daughter in law Kathy brought her horse, Dakota, down to this farm. The man who sold her the horse brought the horse, Dakota, down to the farm. He looked at the pasture rolling up to Shenandoah National Park and then Sky Line Drive and said, "This horse is going to think he is in 'horse heaven.'"

Getting back to early agricultural pursuits, I bought one-hundred chicks and put them in the basement (This was permitted by my mother). Of course chickens go peep, peep. My sister and Alice Rawley, her friend, would bring in their boyfriends. They would ask, "What is that peep, peep about?" "Oh, it's my little brother's chickens in the basement."

At that time my sister Elaine complained to my mother, "You let that boy do anything he wants to." My mother said, "When he is working on these projects, I know where he is and the agricultural projects are constructive." She was so right, compared to what some youths get into nowadays. Vic Beale and Ben Dobbins, both teachers, came down to see the chickens. The pony was also housed in the garage next to my sister's bedroom giving her a reason to complain: the smell of pony manure. My sister never did care for animals of any type. However, later in life, we became very close to each other. We will talk about this later. She was high on education.

Another agricultural pursuit of mine was trading these chickens for hogs. I built a hog house and fence on a neighbor's land by the railroad tracks. They never got out as the fence was buried one foot in the ground and nailed to a board. As I recall, they did all right. Roy Chase, my cousin, hauled the hogs for me.

At one time my good friend Chuck Gibson went in with me on raising and selling sweet corn. Why he wanted to do this I cannot understand as he was a member of the wealthiest family in Greenville. Ben Dobbins would let us take time off from school to work in the gardens. Perhaps his father wanted him to have some practical business training. My mother said that his grandfather, Frank Gibson, ran a clothing store selling neck ties on the street before he established the Gibson Refrigerator Plant. I have included his picture.

It was said that the Gibson Refrigerator Plant was the largest refrigerator plant in the world before its demise. Chuck Gibson, my friend, was the president of the graduating class of 1937. What a loyal friend—that may have been a problem as a number of his friends worked for him at the plant. He told me when he was negotiating with White Motor Co. that it was like a room at the top. My understanding is that high commercial interest rates on loans caused him to lose control. Electrolux eased Chuck out because he would not fire his friends. He had a costly divorce and ended up selling real estate with his new wife. He suffered a devastating stroke being only able to talk by aid of a computer. He was our best man at Janet and my wedding on October 7, 1950. He deserved better.

Chapter IV

Junior & Senior High School

Let us move on to junior high school, which was a productive time. Lefty Robinson, our physical education instructor, said, "We are going to have a boxing tournament. I do not care what your mother's position is—you are going to box." We boxed according to weight. I was classified as a lightweight. I won the lightweight championship; however that last bout with Dwight Clock was tough. I was very fast with my hands, and I had good footwork, and I could hit.

My friend Ed Sharpe's father Red Sharpe had a garage in which he had boxing gloves. At this time I was about sixteen years old, and could lift a hundred pound bag of fertilizer. A larger, out-of-town boy asked, "Walker do you want to put on the gloves?" I said, "Sure, I will put the gloves on with you."

I was a southpaw, leading with my right. He walked right into a short right jab—it hit him on the chin and he went down and out like a stuck hog. I was afraid I had killed him. He finally got up and said, "Walker, you have one hell of a punch." Upon arriving home, I told my mother, "I think I am a pretty good fighter. I am going out for the Golden Gloves."

She said emphatically, "You are not." That was the end of my boxing. So my sister was wrong. There were some times when my mother put her foot down. What a good decision. If I had gotten down to Detroit, there was a good chance I would have gotten my brains scrambled.

In junior high school we had a student council. I was elected mayor of my junior high school. Ben Dobbin had me address the entire assembly, including the high school. It was an experience that almost caused a leakage. Also on my final eighth grade examination in Mrs. White's class, I had the had the highest grade in arithmetic, a big achievement because there were some very smart kids in that class. That was the half-year class.

The Boy Scouts of America has played an important part in this American's life. In Troop 130 of Greenville, I attained the titles of Life Scout and Senior Patrol Leader. Let us put an asterisk on Senior Patrol Leader. I was Patrol Leader, but, there was some dissension in the ranks—some, not all, claimed I spent too much time on games. Landon Rogers, the Scout Master, removed me as Patrol Leader, but promoted me (kicked me upstairs) to Senior Patrol Leader. My loyal friend Chuck Gibson was the first to tell me what was happening. I threatened to resign. Apparently Landon Rogers had "kicked me upstairs" so he would not lose me. He was disappointed when most of us dropped out at age fifteen with the discovery of girls. He would tell my sister Elaine, "Get Woody back in the Boy Scouts." Later in life I would be, when my boys were Scouts.

In high school, Maxine Sharp informed me that I got the highest score on the final exam in commercial arithmetic. In a later class reunion to which I went—I believe in 1987—she said to me in the company of her husband, Claude, "I had the biggest crush on you in high school." I responded by saying, "Now you tell me." In high school I was elected to student council.

I went out for football—I think I weighed about 85 pounds. The coach had me down for quarterback; that is, third string quarterback. I thought if I am going to be third string, I am getting out of football. I remember Bill Bradley, an Eagle Scout, tried very hard to get me back in to football. In retrospect, it was a very good thing that I did not play football. Why? Because I was not big enough. Some of those kids weighed over 200 pounds. Now I ask you, what happens when 200 pounds hits 85 pounds? It is not like boxing where you compete in you same weight—now that is fair.

In the letter category, letters received were for judging in agriculture at Michigan State and cheerleading. Mert Kraas, a brother of my girlfriend, Dorothy, broke a shoulder in football. In those days, the boys were the cheerleaders. Mert said, "Woody let's go out for cheerleader." We practiced some yells and the student body voted on various contestants. We won the cheerleading vote.

Let me say this about high school: I did not study hard at all, but maintained a B+ average, which was good enough to get me accepted at the University of Detroit, a Jesuit university. I had a great time in high school. I had wonderful friends Chuck Gibson, Mert, Ed Sharpe, Bud Ritzema and more too numerous to mention. We attended all the proms and dances. I was in the senior assembly, which was a great success. The class of 1937 voted me the "best-looking boy." The senior play was a failure; however, I do not normally talk, like Gregory Peck, about my failures.

While in high school my mother married Chris Hansen, a good man, a good citizen, and a hard worker, but a man very different from Craig Walker, my father. My mother thought the sun rose and set on Craig Walker. Chris did not go very far in school. As a teenager, I asked, "Mother are you going to marry this man?" She said, "I certainly am. That Rose Walker, when a widow, had a chance to marry and was talked out of it by one of her children." I said no more.

Our clique in high school, as I said, went to all of the school dances. Ed Sharpe, my friend, was always able to get an auto as his dad, Red Sharpe owned a garage and a Dodge-Plymouth dealership. Ed said, "Chris Hansen has just bought a new 1935 Dodge. How about you getting a car for a change?" My mother asked Chris for permission for me to drive the car to the prom. Chris said, "Well, he will not get it." My mother said, "He gets the car or we are through tonight."

I got the car that night and any other time I wanted it. I see it now; this was an omen of later things to come. I guess Chris saw where he ranked. We will talk about that and the Michigan farm soon.

For a teenager I was not a speed demon or a wild driver. I do recall, though, we had gone to Belding after a dance. Claude Chittick was driving a 1935 Ford. We opened the cars up. There were no cars on the road. The Dodge would only go eighty miles-per-hour. He zoomed by me like I was standing still.

About this time a local farmer who was just outside of town by the name of Wayne had been deer hunting. He came home to see a man stealing his chickens in a bag. The man started to run with the chickens down a decline. He shot at him, meaning to hit him in the leg. The man was going downhill and he was hit in the upper body and killed. It was his hired man. Wayne said, "I would have given him the chickens." He was tried in the local court—the jury acquitted him. Remember, this was depression times and Wayne took it very hard.

When I was fifteen years old, I took a job in a local barbershop owned by Jennings Large. I feel this was a mistake, but remember again, it was depression time and he solicited me for the job. I did learn a lot about human nature. In 1934 the Detroit Tigers were a great team. Jennings said, "You put twenty-five cents in a jar when the Tigers lose, and I will put twenty-five cents in a jar when the Tigers win. We will divide it at the end of the year."

The Tigers started winning. Jennings was putting in more than I was putting in the jar. He reneged on the deal. We had a love/hate relationship. I later sold him my shotgun—a double-barrel hammerless. He retired. My cousin Virginia said he committed suicide by killing himself with a shotgun.

I hope it was not my gun that I had sold him years ago. However, for any friction we had, I now forgive him.

The barbers played a trick on me with a local horse trader. They sold a mule to me cheap—one of the barbers said he would furnish the feed, etc. When I went out there he handed me a shovel and said the mule was dead. He wanted to give me a ride back. I told him I would not ride with a crook. I reported it the next morning to a local attorney, Floyd Winters. Of course it was a voidable contract as I was a minor. I never took that track though, as I dealt as though I were an equal asking for no sympathy. Remember, my father died when I was eight years of age.

Chapter V

1939-1943: College

My sister and Ed Woodruff, a great brother-in-law invited me to stay with them. It wasn't the best way to go to college, but it's the way I did it.) The tuition was one hundred dollars a semester. Elaine said, "You did not study in high school. Wait until you take French in college." The first grade I got was an "A" in French. Not bad for coming off the farm. I lost one-year's worth of college credit due to a lack of two years of foreign language in high school.

I went down to Detroit with Jack Pearl who played fullback for the University of Detroit. He was not that big. He said there was a vast difference between high school football and college football. The great Gus Dorais was the coach at that time. I was asked to join two social fraternities. I turned them down. Elaine urged me to join them. I said I was working and trying to get good grades. I was a reporter for the college newspaper.

In the summer of 1941, we had moved to Redford, a suburb of Detroit. The young girl next door invited me to her high school graduation. My sister insisted I go. That summer she wrote me a letter to Greenville about every day, telling my sister we were going to marry and have three children—it never happened.

Jobs During the Summer of 1940 and 1941

I worked at Federal Mogul Corp. This company came to Greenville to make bearings for Detroit automobiles. Mr. Johnson, the superintendent, said he did not hire part-time workers. I talked him into it, but said I would go back to college in the fall to study for law. I was a filer making forty cents an hour.

Mr. Johnson said I was his fastest and best filer. The bearings were formed by punch presses. I saw men go out of there with fingers off. I made up my mind that I would not take that job. The foreman did come around and said, "Walker, I want to put you on the punch press." I said, "I prefer not to take the risk." He immediately went to Mr. Johnson, I guess to fire me, and I was prepared for that. Mr. Johnson said, "Woodrow, go back to your filing." Of course, my name was mud with the foreman from then on.

I went back to the University of Detroit in September of 1940. Mr. Johnson said, "Woodrow, you stay right here with us and I will get you deferment right through the war. You will go to the top of this corporation." I said, "Mr. Johnson, I told you I was going back to college for law and that is what I am going to do. I know I am going into the military and this is what I want to do. I really want to get a degree first."

War Clouds from 1939-1941

In the spring of 1941 a Marine lieutenant came to the campus to recruit for the Platoon Leaders Class. This was for me. The football players could not pass because of some ailments. I passed everything, physical and mental, and had very good grades. There were only two left: myself and another student smaller than me. He took the other man.

I came back to the house very much down and Elaine was grinning like a Cheshire cat. I wondered, "What is the matter with her?" Now I know, the platoon leader was one of the first casualties and I probably would not be writing this history if I had prevailed. However, I later qualified as a sharp shooter in the Michigan ROTC and an expert rifleman in the regular Army. If he had known what an excellent shot I was as well as a tough and skilled boxer, and farm boy, I bet he would have taken me.

In 1941 I transferred from the University of Detroit to the University of Michigan to take military training. I asked the admission clerk at the University of Michigan if there were any questions. She said, "None. You have demonstrated that you can do good college work." However, I lost quite a bit of credit in the transfer.

I rented a room in Ann Arbor with a roommate taking engineering. The roommate was also a short-order cook at the Colonnade, a restaurant on State Street.

I did very well in the basic Michigan ROTC, receiving A and B grades. I received a sergeant rating because I could play the bugle in the fancy marching ROTC Drum and Bugle Corps. We played in football games. We were very popular.

My roommate tested me by coming up behind me for a wrestling match. I was surprised but got a headlock on him, and with my shoulder against his head he had, to go down with me on top with my knees on his arms. He said, "You are strong—you do not look that strong." I said, "You would be strong, too, if you worked on a farm for two years." There was nothing hostile about it. He did not test me again.

My roommate got me a job as a waiter at the restaurant. We had a hamburger and bowl of soup for lunch when the boss was there. When he was not there we had steak sandwiches and a milk shake.

In March of 1943, the Enlisted Reserve Corps for which I had signed up were called up for active duty. The Assistant Dean at Michigan called me into his office and said, "You are off to the war." I said, "Yes."

He said, "Mr. Walker we can give you credit for almost all of your University of Detroit subjects and match them with the University of Michigan subjects and with a pro-rated amount for this semester. You now have enough credits to graduate with your class in June." However, I was in Camp Roberts, California at that time getting basic training. I really wanted that degree to show that I had accomplished something if I did not come back. Can you believe with all my setbacks—the one year of college credit lost in French for high school qualification, a huge loss of credits from transferring from the University of Detroit to University of Michigan, and a lack of financial backing (my father had died when I was 8)—I still graduated from University of Michigan in three and a half years? You will see in the next chapter that I will see plenty of overseas, wartime duty in the fortieth Infantry Division.

The financing of my college education was accomplished by these methods:

1. Selling my livestock from the Michigan farm.
2. Working part-time at college, and full-time in the summer.
3. Receiving a loan from Charles Miller, President of the Commercial Bank in Greenville. The bank note was cosigned by the great Dr. Weaver and my mother. In a later chapter you will learn how I helped pay off this note in a bizarre way. I was ahead of the times for student loans. I still have the bank note copy marked *Paid*.
4. Working at a YMCA for the University of Detroit.
5. Help from my sister Elaine with whom I stayed.
6. My good mother did what she could—I would send home clothes, which she would wash and send back.
7. Working at the University of Michigan Library.

While working in the stacks the U. of M. Library I noted the volume *Who's Who in America*. I thought how great it would be to included in that book. Little did I dream that I would someday be included. Here is a copy of how it appears in the 2009 Volume:

WALKER, WOODROW WILSON, retired lawyer, real estate investor, farmer, b. Greenville, Mich., Feb. 19, 1919;s. Craig Walker and Mildred Chase; m. Janet K. Keiter, Oct. 7, 1950; children: Jonathan Woodrow; William Craig; Elaine Virginia; B.A. U Mich 1943; LLB Cath U. 1950 Bar D.C. U.S. Supreme Ct. 1958, Va. 1959. Operator family farm, 1937-39; dir. Libr. of Congress Fed. Credit Union, 1957-60; atty. Am law div. legis. reference Libr. Congress, Washington, 1951-60; pvt. practice, Arlington, Va., 1960-2000. Counsel, bd. dirs. Calvary Found., Arlington, 1970-85, first pres., 1972; judge moot ct. George Mason Law Sch., 1986, Columbus Law Sch., 2007, Cath. U., 2007; owner-operator Walker Farm Front Royal, Va., 1972–. Co-author rsch. publs. for U.S. Govt.; featured in Washington Post. V.p. Jefferson Civic Assn., Arlington, 1955-61; pres. Nellie Custis PTA, Arlington, 1960-61; sec. Arlington County Bd. Equalization Real Estate Assessment, 1962, chmn. 1963; troop com. chmn. of honor Boy Scouts Sam., 1964-69, life scout, sr. patrol leader troop 131; mem. Arlington County Pub. Utilities Commn., 1964-66, vice chmn., 1965-66; pres. Betchler Class Adult Sunday Sch., Calvary United Meth. Ch., Arlington, 1965. With U.S. Army, 1943-45, PTO. Cited for notable deed in conduct of his legal duties Washington Post, 1996. Mem. ABA, Arlington County Bar Assn., Va. Farm Bur., Va. Cattlema's Assn. Independent. Methodist. Home and Office: 2822 Ft Scott Dr Arlington VA 2202-2307

Chapter VI

Army Service and World War II Duty

You have learned from the chapter on college that I took two years basic of ROTC at the University of Michigan—not enough for a commission requiring four years. I was also in the Enlisted Reserve Corps of that university from August of 1942 to March of 1943.

In March of 1943 the entire enlisted Reserve Corps of the University of Michigan was called to active duty. Most of them went to Camp Roberts, California, for basic training, including yours truly. We were sent to California in sleeping coaches. We stopped at Howard Johnson for meals. Wait till you see how we traveled on furlough.

Basic training was a grueling thirteen weeks. There, they would get you up at 3 A.M. to climb hills. Then there was a twenty-mile hike with the full field pack. I managed to go the route. Big guys dropped out and said they could go no further. Camp Roberts was a semi-desert so we were trained not to drink water. My two years at the farm served me well for the physical training.

Let me say something about the training sergeant in charge of our company: he knew his guns and he knew how to drill a platoon, having done it many times. However, I thought he was ignorant, showing it when he said, "If I were in combat and the lieutenant did something I did not like, the Lieutenant would get a bullet." Most of these recruits were 18 year olds. I was older. I thought that was a terrible thing to say to these impressionable young men. I hoped and prayed that none of them would carry out his advice.

We had a soldier from Kentucky named Smith who did not have very much education. He would be one of the last ones out for retreat with his shirttail hanging out. But let me tell you this: when he got on the firing range he was hitting bullseyes left and right. He qualified as an Expert Rifleman. One other soldier in this training company to my knowledge qualified as an Expert Rifleman—namely, yours truly. My hunting experience in Michigan paid off.

I had a BB gun at eight, a .22 rifle at twelve or thirteen, a twenty-gauge shotgun at fourteen, and a twelve-gauge, double-barrel, hammerless Lefever shotgun in high school. Is it no wonder that I was an Expert Rifleman in the regular army and a sharp shooter in ROTC? Now do you see why the marine lieutenant made a mistake in not taking me in the Marine Platoon Leader's Class at the University of Detroit? I guess he thought I was too much the student.

There was a large Polish recruit from Wisconsin who took a liking to me – and called me J.J. Walker. For some reason this ignorant Drill Sergeant got down on him and said he was going to mop the ground with him. I would have liked to have seen that little banty rooster tackle that big Polish soldier.

When basic training was over we were given two weeks furlough. I told you earlier that I would tell you about the transportation. It was on a cattle train (at least that is what we called it). The passenger cars looked like nineteenth-century ones. We stood up most of the way. We were a far cry from the University of Michigan students, who went out to Camp Roberts in Pullman cars and ate at Howard Johnson restaurants.

Visit to Uncle H.N. – Mabel Omsbee

While taking basic training, I visited my Uncle H.N. and Aunt Mabel at Capitola, California. Their one son, Sydney was a navigator on a Mitchell Bomber. I have to say, they could not brag enough about Sydney. He was a fine young man. They talked about how much money he made, etc. It made me feel like a proletariat. I will tell you later about Sydney and my aunt and uncle.

While home I visited my old high-school girlfriend Dorothy. She said, "You ought to be able to get something out of this." At this time, my mother was living in a cottage at Turk Lake. I believe my mother moved around so much because my father's early death unsettled her. While in service, I took out an allotment for my mother. She also had a job for the first time in her life at a potato plant in Greenville.

After returning from the furlough on the "cattle train," we were sent to a port of debarkation. We got on a boat at midnight in San Francisco not knowing where we were being sent. The boat was an old World War I boat, but it was sea worthy. Some of the soldiers got seasick—I never did get seasick. I thought I was being sent over as a "sniper" because of my excellent marksmanship—this was not to be the case. We were sent to the Hawaiian Islands, Honolulu, Oahu. and Schofield barracks. The fortieth was a California National Guard division sent to Hawaii after Pearl Harbor.

28

After a short time at Schofield, eleven of the replacements were called out to go to headquarters. There I was assigned, and there I would stay. As far as I could determine, I was the only one to stay in HQ as such. Some, I believe, went to HQ Company, which did all of the detail work that the prima donnas in HQ did not do, such as KP, latrine, and guard duty. We did guard duty when the division was in combat. I will tell you later about an amusing incident while doing guard duty during combat that involved a talented friend named Kenny.

While in Hawaii I dated a Chinese schoolteacher who had a master's degree. Nothing became of that. We were all taken out of school in December, 1943, to go to Guadalcanal and and later to New Britain Island (known as the South Pacific and the Southwest respectively). We bunkered down on one end of New Britain Island and the Japanese had fifty thousand troops down at the other end at Rabaul. We had control of the air and the sea at this time; I hear that our General, Rapp Brush, wanted to go down and "clean them out." The pentagon said, "No." The Japanese were reduced to raiding gardens for food. One American division immobilized those fifty thousand Japanese without firing a shot. It sounded like a good idea to me.

Let me tell you how I paid off most of my student loan of $150 at the Commercial Bank. Tuition at University of Michigan at that time was sixty dollars per semester for a Michigan resident.

At New Britain Island we lived in tents. It was decided we would have a poker game with eight men and two decks of cards. The limit was a floren, which was at that time thirty-two cents. At that time I was the lowest-ranking man and the new kid on the block. I am sure these high-ranking noncoms (master and technical sergeants) thought that this green soldier knew nothing about poker. Well, I cannot tell you what kind of luck I had. I would have three aces and draw the fourth one. I would have the makings of a straight flush, and get dealt the card I needed for a it. They were throwing their caps on the floor and swearing, saying they had never seen such luck. Needless to say, I cleaned them out.

The next morning I went down to the Post Exchange and applied the entire winning to the $150 loan at the Commercial Bank. I never gambled again in the service, and we never had another poker game. I guess the HQ personnel did not want to play with me again.

Life at New Britain Island was dull. The natives had elephantiasis and we were told not to associate with them. Of course we did not.

We were told by the colonel to work half days. We could go swimming in the afternoon. One time when we saw fins in the water, we made a beeline for shore, splashing all the way. Little did we know at the time about the great white sharks off the coastline of Australia, which is close to New Britain Island.

I recall that some nurses landed on the island and Major Wilson asked me if I would walk one of them home in the evening, which I did.

Life on New Britain Island was uneventful. The line troops were in constant training getting ready for what was coming.

Come it did. In December of 1944, we were loaded onto one huge luxury passenger ship. I am not sure how many troops were on the luxury passenger line. We had no escort. It was said that it was too fast for Japanese submarines. I was not too sure about that.

Somebody threw a candy wrapper overboard and one of the naval officers shouted over the loudspeaker, "Do you want to get this ship sunk? Do not throw anything overboard!" Besides that, they were dropping depth bombs, which meant that Japanese submarines were in the area. Sinking this huge luxury liner with all these fortieth infantry troops aboard, including the HQ personnel, would have been a feather in the cap of the Japanese. At this point and time, the Japanese needed a feather in their cap.

With the possibility that this ship could be sunk by Japanese torpedoes, and HQ personnel including yours truly killed, I came to the conclusion that if we got torpedoed, there would be no escape. I further concluded that there was not a thing I could do about it. If my time was coming up "so be it." I would be going to my maker.

We headed for the invasion of Luzon Island in the Philippines. I slept like a baby all the way up there. I will tell you later that my premonition turned out to be correct.

When we arrived at our destination, there were all kinds of ships pouring into this area. aircraft carriers, naval war ships; I was told that there were close to a thousand ships. I have no accurate information on the number. The big naval guns raked the coastline. I understand from a downed pilot the airships had been raking the Japanese coastline earlier. The pilot told me, "You guys had it kind of easy coming in here." Little did he know about what happened to the compartment of HQ personnel of the luxury ship.

The G-3 personnel were one of the first waves to go to shore. There was no opposition. I understand that the Japanese Army commander decided to retreat when he saw all of those ships off the coast. However, it was reported that if he had known that there were not that many army troops, he would have made a stand.

Upon landing, we immediately dug foxholes. Later I noticed men coming ashore covered with oil. I thought they had been working on motor vehicles as mechanics. No, they were HQ personnel from the adjutant general's office. A Japanese motor torpedo boat had come in speedily and launched a torpedo into the very compartment that G-3 had vacated to come in on the first wave. I was told it was all hell down there as the water poured in on our compartment. That there was a fight to get out. My premonition about a torpedo coming in on this luxury troop ship turned out to be correct. There were only a few pesky Japanese planes harassing us at this time.

From here the fortieth Division was heavily equipped for combat along with the Ohio thirty-seventh Division for the duel against the Japanese Army. There were others in this drive also, which I cannot relate. The Army went by corps.

I read an article in the *The Washington Post* stating that the Luzon Campaign was one of the most decisive victories in the Philippine Campaign.

General Kruger was the commander of the Sixth Army. Of course, the great General McArthur was overall commander of the Army, Navy, and Marines. He went down to our headquarters twice. I missed him both times. He reportedly said the fortieth were his best troops. I did get to see him later in life when he had a major setback in his brilliant military career, which I will tell you about later.

It was a fast-moving drive. We were in trucks and it was, "Hurry up, hurry up." I remember going through Tarlac. The Japanese had set fire to the town. It was still burning.

We hardly had time to eat C rations. I am sure we lost some weight. We went down the same railroad toward Bataan that the Japanese had gone down after Pearl Harbor. After Pearl Harbor, the Japanese had control of the sea, air, and land. What a dramatic change at this time.

Can I tell you about an incident that occurred on Luzon Island. Major Wilkins and I at this time were in GI. Also in this section was a Sergeant who stated he had an IQ of 160. He had, in civilian life, worked for National Cash Register and was indeed a very intelligent individual.

The major decided we should look for a new bivouac area. The major and Sergeant Ackerman were in a Jeep, ready to go to the front lines. I said I wanted to go as well. The Major asked, "Sergeant Walker, do you want to go?" Here was a chance for me to get to the front lines. I said, "Yes Sir. We were off. We came upon the frontline troops in battle formation. One of the line troops asked this (and I am going to give you a direct quote): "Have you seen any Japs yet?" We said, "No." This time the bullets whistled over our heads. We all hit the ditch. We then proceeded to look for a bivouac.

We found an old abandoned Philippine warehouse. We were prowling around in there and it occurred to me later that if there were any Japanese soldiers in there, we could have been easily knocked off.

The major threat in World War II was in the European theatre. Most of the materials and men were being sent to Europe. My understanding at the time was that General McArthur was to fight a holding action until the European threats could be secured.

General McArthur successfully went on the offensive. He said upon leaving the Philippines, "I will return." In the Philippines those of us in in HQ slept in hammocks. I heard that the Japanese would come in the night and cut the hammock in half with their swords. I slept in the hammock with a loaded carbine at my side, determined to fire through the hammock if confronted with Japanese soldiers.

I had told you earlier that HQ personnel did not do guard duty. Well, we did do guard duty in combat. I was doing guard duty with a clerk named Kenny. It was a moonlit night and you could see pretty well. I asked, "Kenny, what would you do if you saw one of those slant eyes sneaking around here?" Kenny said, "I would faint." He was a talented clerk—not a soldier. He was such a good clerk, the HQ of the Sixth Army took him.

When we got back to fortieth Division headquarters, HQ the Division commander, Major General Rapp Brush was waiting for us. He gave the major holy hell up one side and down the other. The major general said, "Don't you ever take these men up to the front lines! Their job is back here." I felt so sorry for my friend, Major Wilkins. I wanted to tell the General I volunteered but thought that with the mood the General was in that this would not have been a good idea. Upon reflection, I am sure this was correct.

The division was divided into regiments and went from island to island to clean out the Japanese. You know the Japanese soldier was taught to never surrender even if the military situation were hopeless.

HQ was on the island of Panay, in Iloilo City. While on that island, the original cast of *Oklahoma* arrived to entertain the troops. I was given a ticket by a soldier I did not know. While I was attending that performance, the word came out that a small bomb had been dropped on a Japanese city, destroying the whole city. This was hard to believe but it turned out to be true.

An interesting note here is that Fred Bock, a Greenville high school graduate, and an all A student, was the navigator of the B-29 called *Bock's Boxcar* for this mission.

Let me regress here a little bit. Our literature teacher for the Class of 1937 was a Mr. Garter who had travelled to Manchuria earlier and who had witnessed the cruelty of the Japanese army at that time to the Chinese. He said to us teenage boys at that time, "I would like to see how you drugstore cowboys would stand up to the Japanese Army."

Well, I can tell you that the Greenville boys did very well in World War II. Fred Bock is one example. And, of course, the American soldiers, and all who served, stood up very well. Another theory was that the American combatant could not survive in the tropical jungles. The armed service did a super job of keeping everyone healthy. Mr. Garter was a very good teacher; he could have taught in college.

While in the Philippines, the assistant division commander, a brigadier general conducted a general inspection of HQ personnel. He came to me, taking an inordinate amount of time going over my rifle. I was sure he was finding something wrong. Finally he asked, "Sergeant, How long have you had this rifle?"

I said, "Ever since I was assigned to division HQ."

At this time the General said, "Sergeant, this is the best cared-for rifle in the whole division." I thought that was quite a compliment. You could look down the barrel - it was like mirror. The stock was highly polished – this goes back to my hunting experience in Michigan.

While on Luzon Island, a captured Japanese lieutenant who spoke very good English said, "The war is over. We are defeated." Now here was one Japanese lieutenant who believed in surrendering if the situation were hopeless. We also received a lecture by an American lieutenant who had studied the psychology of the Japanese at Yale University. He said, "If the Japanese choose to defend the homeland, they would fight to the last man and woman and child. If they decided to surrender, they would lay down their arms and that would be the end of the war."

With the war in Europe over, the fortieth Division was staging, getting ready to invade the Japanese homeland. Troops from Europe were assembling, getting ready to come over. Russia came into the Pacific war. The Japanese situation was getting hopeless. Fortunately, the Japanese Emperor had the good sense to surrender, as he knew it was the best interest of the Japanese and, incidentally, the United States and its allies. If we had invaded Japan, I may not be writing right now.

The war was over—now we were going home. Not so fast—orders came down that the fortieth Infantry was going to open up Korea. The division— or at least HQ—was a pretty sad bunch of soldiers. When the ship came into the Korean harbor, everything in the city was battened down. I will tell you later why the city was battened down, as related by our Korean neighbors.

Russia was in the Pacific War for about two days. In the peace negotiations, we divided Korea, Vietnam, and some Japanese islands. In my humble opinion, this should never have happened. At the end of World War II, we had about twenty-million veteran men under arms; the largest navy, air force, army, and marine corps; and the first atom bomb the world had ever known. Why not stand firm? Perhaps in doing so we could have avoided the Korean War and the Vietnam War. We won the war and lost peace, again. I know we had agreed to this.

I was in South Korea for about six weeks. I got out early after thirty-three months of active service; about thirty of those were overseas. We got double credit for being in a combat area. About fifty soldiers came back home on a freighter. The food was great. There was nothing to do but read. We came down the Pacific coast and through the Panama Canal. It took thirty days to make it to Norfolk.

We stopped off in Panama City because we were permitted to get off the ship for a beer. I went into a tavern with two other soldiers from Michigan. Both of these men were from the same small town. One was a big guy, the other a small guy. The small guy had too many drinks, saying some things to the big guy that he should not have. I could see that the big guy was getting madder and madder. The little guy said, "Yeah, you really scare me." At this time the big guy was about to clobber him. I stepped between them and said, "Come on guys, let's get back on the ship." That cooled things off.

The next morning onboard the ship, the big guy came up to me and said, "Woody, I am so glad that you stepped between us. I was ready to hit him. I would have always been sorry." I told him, "I could see that was what you were going to do."

We came into Norfolk, Virginia and were discharged at Camp Grant. I was asked to sign up for the reserves. I said, "No, I will take the honorable discharge." I am sure if I had a commission I would have served in the Korean War.

It was good to get back to my hometown of Greenville. To see old high school friends, especially Chuck Gibson, Ed Sharpe, Bur Ritzema, and many others. We had parties.

Bill and Anne married at Calvary Methodist Church. February 23, 1985.

My daughter-in-law Kathy receiving her AB degree from Marymount University Summa Cum Laude, 2008.

Early 1920s. L to R: Brother Ralph, Sister Elaine, Father Craig, Woody, Brother Bill, Mother.

Jonathan N., grandson on Black Walnut logs some Venir, April, 2008, on Walker Farm.

Greenville High School football team. Craig Walker, Woody's father, top row far right, Manager, early 1900s.

Aerial photo of 128 acre Walker Farm.

Wedding Day. Left to right: Robert Keiter, Ginny Mund, Kathy Shaffer, Janet, Woody, Charles Gibson, Pres. Gibson Refrigerator, Ed Sharpe Ted Keiter. Oct. 7, 1950, Toledo, Ohio.

Kindergarten, Parl St. School, 1924, Woody, 2nd from left bottom row. Five years old.

Janet, July, 1949

South Korean Embassy party, Left Janet, Capt. Shinn, Mrs. Shinn, Woody. Early 1960s.

My daughter, Elaine, on graduation from high school.

Woody. Elected Mayor of Junior High school, 13 years old.

Our first house. 601 S. 19th St. ARL

End of year cattle going to stock yards.

Woody, Univ Detroit, Candidate for Marine Platoon Leader's Class, March 27, 1941. Soph.

Woody at work in his law office.

Royal Haven. Janet's care home during her illness.

Woody entering war. Chicago, 24 years old.

VIRGINIA WALKER

"Forget-me-not."

Most Dignified Girl
Secretary '33
Newspaper '34
Orchestra '33, '34, '35, '36
Treasurer '37

WOODROW WALKER

"You are liked because it is said that you are handsome."

Best Looking Boy
Band '34, '35
Student Council '34
Judging '34
Senior Play '37
Annual Staff '37
CHEER LEADER 34-35

RUTH WILKINSON

"Sincere and cheerful."

JENNIE ZIEGENFUSS

"Oh..."

Married, Oct. 7, 1950. Walking down aisle. Baptist church. Janet and Woody.

Fort Scott Park accomplished by urging of Jefferson Civic League.

Keiter family at Williamsburg. L to R: Fred, Kathy, Bob, Janet, Ted.

Picture of Woody - Arlington County Bar Association. 2007.

Woody, June 1950. Graduate from law school and passed D.C. bar.

2822 Ft. Scott Dr. Arl., VA 22202. May 2008.

Woody, President, 3rd from right, back row. Sunday school class two years. Gen. Faw, first from left, back row, teacher.

Woody and Janet, Easter Sunday, 1950. Washington.

Farm house. May, 2008. Walker Family Farm.

Walker Family Farm. L to R: Cousin Virginia, her son Ralph Wood, valedictorian of the 1958 Greenville High School class, Barney Wood, Janet and Woody.

Walker Family: Left to right: Billy, Jonathan, Elaine, Janeet and Woody. Early 1960s.

Janet, Secretary to President. American Petroleum Institute. 1950.

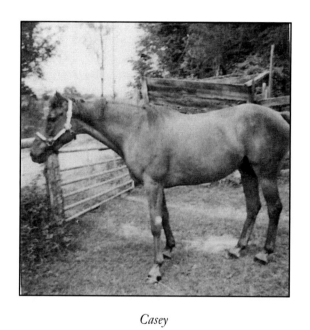

Casey

Marie, Cindy and Woody, April 1991

My oldest son, Jonathan and his bride, Kathy on their honeymoon in Hawaii.

Marvel Rasmussen (now Zona) my friend who suggested this book.

My cousin, Lloyd Walker, longtime mayor of Greenville, and wife, Marcia.

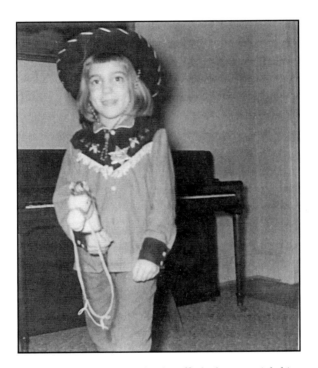

Elaine, daughter, with horse Reddi, sheriff's badge, cowgirl shirt and hat.

Woody, Jan. 1946

Expert rifleman badge.

Holly in the Hills. Owned by Marvel Rosmusen. She is asking 16M. It was built by an orange grove magnate.

Woody and children. July 1960. First year solo law practice. Arlington, VA.

LAWYER
OF THE
MONTH

COMMUTING, STEP BY STEP

U.S. Bankruptcy Trustee Woodrow Walker heads toward his office on soggy Union Street in Old Town Alexandria.

Picture of author taken in 1996 by Washington Post. Author is on way to U.S. Bankruptcy Trustee Hearing.

Walker Farm barn in July, 2008. Contrast June, 1973.

Walker Farm barn in June 1973. See the contrast in 2008.

Daugther, Elaine, with her dad, Woody in sixties on side of our first house.

Picture of Woody in front of Michigan Farm barn, 2007. Now Thompson's Farms.

Frank Gibson, founder of The Gibson Refrigerator, Greenville, Michigan's largest refrigerator in the world at one time. Grandfather Charles Jr.

My friends of the Arlington Bar Association. Bankhead T. Davies and Bankhead Thornton Davies.

Chapter VII

Night Law School

It was my intention to go to law school. I was offered a job in a local drug store, but I turned it down. I went to Washington and interviewed at Columbus Law School on Eighteenth Street, a night law school. I attended five times a week.

I was impressed with Dean Hayden who said, "I think you could do very good work in the legal field." He gave me a series of tests to find out my strengths and talents. He said, "You are red hot in law if you scored ninety-five 95." Ninety-five was higher than the scores of the professors. That gave me encouragement that I was on the right track.

It was my intention to work part time while going to law school. My main objective was to go to law school. I did get a job at Veterans Administration— for twenty-four hours a week. Veterans Administration wanted to give me a GS-5 but full time. I turned it down.

I found a room near the law school on Fifteenth Street. It was a small room, but clean and quiet. It suited my needs. A Mrs. Riley had two other rooms. One of the roommates was a young man working for the government by the name of Menno Brake, whose cousin, D. Hale Brake was the treasurer of Michigan.

There was also a boarding house on Rhode Island Avenue where you could buy dinners. Again, this suited me just fine by separating the boarding house from my room, making for more privacy for a serious law student. One block over from my room was the Foundry Methodist Church; which turned out to be the most important turning point in my life. I will explain this later.

Indeed, on the first grading period I had two As and a B. I was second in the class to a naval captain. I knew I was on my way. One of the professors said, "You are going to make an excellent lawyer."

A law school friend of mine and I were invited to join a legal fraternity. I thought joining it would aid a legal career. However, we were told that the fraternity did not admit Jewish law students. Paul and I walked out. I never did join a legal fraternity.

Another incident of interest occurred when another student and I were walking home from the law school. We came upon a scene in which a young lady was yelling that her purse had been stolen. The culprit was running down the street. I said to John, a former professional boxer, "Let's go get him." I thought, between John and me, we could handle him. John said, "Hold on, Woody." He talked to the young lady.

I said later, "John, why did you not want to go after that guy?" John with a cooler, more mature head, said, "Woody, you do not know how that robber wasn't armed. He may have had a gun or a knife." I thought later that John was quite correct.

Two of the night law students were a husband and wife team. The husband had been a clerk of the circuit court of a Missouri county. I did not know this until later. President Truman had brought him here to hold an important position in the Internal Revenue Service. You will see later how financially successful he became in later life, but not necessarily from law practice (although they did have a successful law practice).

One lady from Oklahoma and her daughter were boarders at the boarding house. The owner of the boarding house said to me, "Now, this daughter would make a very good wife." Perhaps so, but at this point and time I was not interested in marrying. The daughter's mother told me, "Woodrow, one of these days a little girl is going to get a hold of you and you will not know what hit you." This statement turned out to be prophetic.

I stuck with the regime of working part time while going to night law school. In addition, I attended summer law school at nights as I was in a hurry to get out into the real world. Because I was on the G-I Bill, my mother received an allotment as she did when I was in the service. I managed to keep up my ten-thousand dollar Army life insurance policy. You will see that this was an excellent personal financial move later.

Brake and I would go swimming in the summertime in the Chesapeake Bay. He had purchased a Chevrolet Coupe. I did not have a car; I was using public transportation.

The Foundry Methodist Church sponsored a group called the Foundry Pairs. It was made up primarily of single returning veterans and young single women who worked for the federal government. The church also sponsored a Tuesday-night open house. Couples gathered on the second floor of a mansion to dance to the music of a record player! I dated a number of the young ladies, but didn't click with any of them. In my senior year, I met Janet Keiter, from Toledo, Ohio. It was not love at first sight, but from the very first date it seemed like we were meant for each other. She was holding down a very challenging job as a secretary to the president of the American Petroleum Institute in Washington, D.C.

Jumping way ahead here—we were married fifty-eight years ago, on October 7, 1950. We never called each other names. We never thought about, mentioned, or discussed separation or divorce. We never had an argument over money. We both had input on major purchases, except for one: our first house, and it was I who jumped the gun. Janet left the financial management to me because she believed I was better at it than she was. We did do well.

One thing we did not agree on was her driving. When she was backing out of the carport during her driver's training course, she took off the door on her side. She finally decided on her own that driving was not for her.

I told you about the lady from Oklahoma who made the prediction. Well, Janet and I were walking down Fourteenth Street one night in late 1949 when we encountered this woman and her daughter. By reading the mother's body language, it was obvious to me that her prophecy was accurate—she acted as though Janet did not exist. Her prediction came true. That I would meet some young lady and I would not know what hit me.

Some look at the first shot at the Bar exam while going to law school as a trial run. I didn't pass the D.C. Bar the first time I took it. It was 1949, and I was still in law school. However, I was told by one of the examiners that I came very close. There were so many veterans taking the Bar that the examiners passed only fifty percent of those who sat for the exam.

Columbus Law School held its graduation in June of 1950. Janet insisted that we go. She bought a red suit, and looked very beautiful and petite, and very much the secretary to the president of American Petroleum. After graduation and my second attempt at the Bar, Janet and I boarded the B&O train for a trip back to the Midwest. Janet wanted to stop in Toledo so I could meet her family. Well aware that when you marry the girl you marry the family, I agreed that this was a good idea. The family repeatedly asked me about my intentions. I answered truthfully that I would have to wait and see how it came out in the Bar.

I traveled from Toledo to Greenville, where I caught up with my best friend, Chuck Gibson. He took me to the country club and we had a drink with the Prudential Insurance man. He and Chuck agreed that I (yours truly), would probably make about fifty-thousand dollars a year as a Washington lawyer. It seemed like pie in the sky to me at the time. I never imagined that in time we would far exceed that amount.

Generally, I follow the advice of Gregory Peck, who said, "I never talk about my failures."

So in June of 1950, older but wiser, I took Frank Smith's Bar review prior to my second attempt at the Bar Exam. I was a good student. In fact, Frank Smith said that I was his best. He gave us a list of recent cases that he thought would be referenced on the Bar. I went to the law library of the Library of Congress and studied them. Lo and behold, a number of the exam questions, particularly concerning real property, did come from those cases. While sitting in the exam for three days at Georgetown, I could actually visualize the cases while I answered the questions. As I told Frank Smith how I answered some of the hard questions, he said, "You passed."

In the meantime, Janet could not understand why I had not yet proposed. The reason was that I had made up my mind to finish my legal education before getting married. The day the Bar results were published in the paper, Janet called, being the first to inform me that I had passed. Brake immediately went down to the drugstore and bought a paper.

Chapter VIII

Marriage and House

That night I asked Janet to marry me. The next morning she called me up, saying come over. She made me repeat the question. I asked her if she wanted it notarized.

The woman I married was a very talented writer of poetry, and an actress as well. Two of her poems will follow.

I mentioned jumping the gun on a major purchase without Janet's input. And I do mean a major purchase. I graduated from law school and passed the Bar without incurring any debt. The debt from the A.B. Degree had been paid mostly from the poker game and I had money in the bank. Janet had been thrifty and also had money in the bank, and suggested that we pool our assets. I liked the idea. Because I had served in the war, spent two years in a farm store and factory; and attended about seven years of college, I felt that I was behind my contemporaries. I was motivated to become a homeowner. Brake advised us to get an apartment.

I looked in the paper and saw a bungalow for sale in Arlington. Having no debt, no job, and no car, I took the bus to Arlington Realty on Wilson Boulevard. A Mr. Matson, a mature salesman from Chicago, showed me the house. It had an apartment attached to its side, and a broad expanse of land next to the apartment. It was listed at $12,950.

I said, "I'll take it." He looked at me and asked, "Boy, can you cut this?" I replied, "I can cut it." I figured that the rent from the apartment would help pay the mortgage if times got tough. I also thought the broad expanse of land to the side would be valuable and that someday a new house could be built on it. I was right on both points, even though the broad expanse of land turned out to be not so broad. More on that later.

I broke the news to Janet that we needed to go to Arlington Realty to sign the contract and pay five-hundred dollars in earnest money. She seemed a little rattled by the rapid chain of events. The five-hundred dollars came out of Janet's checking account! However, she didn't object, trusting that I knew what I was doing. Mind you, I still did not have a job.

To finance our purchase, we secured a GI. loan at four-percent APR That was big money in those days, especially to Janet and me.

Here are the two poems of hers I promised you.

Words Are Not Enough

How can I put in words how much I love you
    When words are merely blunt and broken tools
With which I try to carve a living statue
    Of gleaming marble, set with precious jewels.

The cold and careful phrasing of a sonnet
    Cannot express the sweetness of your kiss
Nor yet disclose the rose with dew upon it
    Nor sing the wondrous joy of mutual bliss.

The warm and glowing sunshine of your smile, Dear
    Would lose its magic charm and fade away,
If crowded into words and writ on paper,
    E'en as moonlight fades into the dawning day.

As every lover feels that none before him
    Has ever reached the heights that he has climbed;
So every poet knows the lonely anguish
    Of searching for the words which flee his mind.

O, for a thousand tongues to sing your praises;
O, for a thousand words to tell your charms;
Give me a thousand ways to say "I love you,"
And a hundred thousand nights within your arms.

                                   May, 1950

Poem To Woody

You wonder why I love you?
Why does the westwind blow?

87

Why is a child enchanted
With the swirling, feathery snow?
Why do the raindrops drench the earth?
Who paints the sunset's glow?
You wonder why I love you?
Because God wished it so.
How much, Sweet, do I love you?
How high do eagles fly?
How many hundred-thousand stars
Are glittering from on high?
How many tiny grains of sand
In burning deserts lie?
How much, Sweet, do I love you?
How lofty is the sky?

How long, dear, will I love you?
Til life's last tale is told;
Til music's magic charm has fled,
And Mercury's feet are slowed;
Til spring's bright jonquils fail to bloom
Amidst a shower of gold.
How long, Dear, will I love you?
Until the stars grow cold.

March 1950

As for the room and apartment at 1412 Northwest Fifteenth Street, Mrs. Riley, the landlady, had been taking care of an elderly woman and decided to give up the apartment. It had three bedrooms, a bath, a kitchen, and a living room. The furniture was old but there were some good pieces; so nice in fact, the gold mirror is hanging in our living room.

Mrs. Riley said, "I'll sell everything in here to you boys." We accepted. Because Brake had a regular job, he took over the lease. Of course, we shared the expenses and income, because the third bedroom was rented to a sophisticated Englishman.

Now, I tried to find a job to pay the mortgage. It seemed that there were none available. I could type reasonably fast—forty words a minute—and landed a job in the supply office at the Library of Congress.

We were planning a June wedding in 1951, but for some reason, there was a delay with our loan approval. When I asked the Arlington Realty manager Mr. Florance what was causing the holdup he said, "Wedding bells." So we moved the date up to October 7, 1950. In the meantime, Janet was given two showers—one was held by the Foundry Pairs. I took a second, part-time job at Woody's in the luggage department. We met many interesting people.

We were trying to build a three-thousand dollar kitty for our down payment. Lucky for us, the Veterans Administration had negotiated the purchase price down from $12,950 to $12,600.

When I decided to leave the American Law Division to go into private practice, the apartment served its purpose, becoming a source of income during that lean first year.

Today this sounds like peanuts, but it was big bucks to us at that time. It would turn out that this house served not only as a roof over our heads and a home for our children yet to be born, but an investment far beyond my original vision for it. We were fortunate to start out with no debt. It's not unusual for today's law graduate to begin a career with one-hundred-thousand dollars in debt.

A professional legal job opened up in the American Law Division, known at that time as the Legislative Reference Service for the Congress of the United States. It is now known as the Congressional Research Service. I submitted my Form 57, the official application for the job. We needed the salary to pay for the house and future expenses. I was told by Dr. Griffith, then director of the Legislative Reference Service, that there were thirty-five applicants.

The Law Division was a very academic place and the job opening attracted some outstanding potential recruits. The pool was narrowed down to three candidates and I was one of them; later, Dr. Griffith said I was one of two. We were on pins and needles, as you can probably imagine. I really didn't think I would be chosen.

Then, Dr. Griffith came down and said, "we are going to go with you. There are others who have much better résumés than yours, but there is something about you, Woodrow, that we like." Mr. Radigan, the Chief of American Law Division said "he had visited the Columbus Law School and was especially impressed by their law library." This was the break we needed—and jumping the gun to buy the house paid off. However, we did have to call on my good brother-in-law, Ed Woodruff, manager of the Personal Finance Company in Ann Arbor, Michigan, for a one-thousand-dollar loan, with six percent interest, to put us over the top. He borrowed the money from a local Ann Arbor bank to avoid conflict of interest—probably at a better rate. We paid off the loan in short order.

Here is the story of our first car. Next to our house was a housing project in an old brick yard used for temporary housing during the war. A Mr. Ragalie owned the lot next to our lot. In a conversation with him, I predicted the temporary housing was going to be torn down. He said, "Boy, you will be an old man with a white beard before these apartments are torn down." He was wrong—Crystal Apartments, built by Charles Smith, now stand in the old brick yard.

Cars were scarce after the war, but we saw two for sale: a Henry J and a 1940 Plymouth, which had been a taxi cab. We bought the Plymouth for

$250. It had truly been through the war and the motor had been replaced. It broke down quite often.

Now, I had never owned a car (except a Model T when I was a boy) so I had to get a driver's license. I had never taken a driver's training course. I learned everything I knew by sitting in a car with Ed Sharpe. I would ask, "How does the shift work?" And he'd explain, "Like an H," and I asked to try one.

We decided to spend our vacation driving to my childhood home in Greenville, Michigan, and then to Toledo, Ohio, Janet's hometown.

It was an adventure. As we were going down the mountainside in Maryland, I had erroneously shifted to neutral and the brakes gave out. We were going faster and faster—I told Janet, "I have no brakes—the pedal is just flopping up and down!" She said, "Well, do something!" It's funny what flashes through your mind when you are faced with a real life-or-death crisis. I kept hitting the brake pedal hard and releasing it. I thought about putting it in gear, then I thought about driving off the road into the brush until we stopped—a better alternative to arriving at the bottom of the mountain going ninety miles per hour or more. Then, a miracle occurred. The brakes came back.

We took Route 40 and stayed in a motel, making it a two-day trip. By the time we got to Greenville, the muffler had given out. My brother Ralph installed a new one. Jerry Sage, the local chief of police, was known to be an aggressive policeman.

After purchasing the former taxi cab, we painted it blue and nicknamed it the *Blue Monster*. After our close call in the mountains, we decided to call on my old friend Ed Sharpe, whose dad ran Sharpe's Garage and the Pontiac dealership. We were thinking about buying a new car. Ed got into the *Blue Monster*, looked around and asked, "Where did you get this car?" Apparently he didn't think very much of it. Janet said, "We painted it ourselves." He replied, "I can tell." We didn't buy a new car there and had plenty more adventures in the "*Blue Monster*."

Back in Arlington, we found a tenant for the apartment by the name of Jim Clary and his wife, Barbara. He was in the service and later worked for the railroad. One time we were downtown on Fourteen Street crossing Pennsylvania Avenue when the *Blue Monster* went dead. We called Jim and he came down. He had a dog chain and was towing us across Pennsylvania Avenue when the chain broke. Janet was in Jim's car. Jim said, "We just lost Woody." Well, we finally got hooked back up and got the Plymouth to the garage. And that wasn't the last of it. It wasn't long before we'd had it with used cars.

While in Greenville, I decided to take Janet to Crystal Lake Dance Pavilion, a very popular place in the late 1930s. After showing Janet the Michigan farm, we stopped to say hello to Harris Hill, the owner of a country store nearby. As a younger man, I would go to the store in the evening and play cards with Howard Sharpe, Kenneth Mann, and the owner, Harris Hill. During our visit, Harris mentioned that Bert Pearle from Chicago was coming to Crystal Lake and we could dance for a dime. I remembered the excitement of the dance hall and the huge crowds it attracted. So my brother Ralph, his wife Etta, Janet, and I went to Crystal Lake. What a disappointment. The place was deserted, except for a couple of people on the dance floor. Nothing stays the same.

We had a wonderful cat named Gregory. He was a purebred Persian, given to us by Mr. Newman, the British tenant, when we took over the Fifteenth Street apartment. Janet loved cats. Well, he was something else. He grew into a huge cat with huge teeth. As a kitten, he loved to climb the curtains. He moved with us to the Nineteenth Street house, and one afternoon, while on the back porch, he encountered the enemy.

Two small dogs started advancing toward him, obviously expecting Gregory to retreat or seek refuge in a tree. Instead, he bushed out his huge tail and arched his back, shows his teeth and hissed as he advanced on the dogs. Recognizing their tactical error, the dogs turned tail, whimpered, and ran away. The cat had no fear. Another time we took him with us to Columbus and Toledo. He trapped Janet's sister Kathy's neighbor's dog under the car. In Toledo, Janet's mother said he bullied two big yellow cats after escaping from the house. Kathy said she didn't care if he got lost.

The Nineteenth Street house needed work. We did a lot of it. I can't tell you all the improvements that we made. At first, we built a small fence for Jonathan, our first son, but it didn't work. We decided to install a Sears brand chain link fence around the whole property, but that required a survey. The old, rusty wire fence was over several feet of Ragalie's lot as well, so I asked him to help pay for the new fence on the joint property line.

Ragalie asked, "What is wrong with the fence that is already there?" I replied, "It is rusting out and my son could get hurt on it." He refused.

I got some good advice from the surveyor. He suggested that I set my fence two inches inside my property line. That way, the fence was on our property. The neighbor in the back asked for a gate along the rear so his kids could walk through our yard instead of going around the corner. His son was also in the habit of playing football in our side yard. We asked him, "Why don't you play in your own yard?" The reply was, "My dad wants to preserve his lawn." Nevertheless, we had good relations with Ragalie and the neighbor in the back.

The previous owner of the Nineteenth Street house—the husband—did not want to sell, but his wife did. She was a buyer for Woodward & Lothrop and often traveled to New York City. Prior to the settlement, Janet announced that she wanted an automatic washing machine. We bought a Kenmore, and asked Sears to deliver it to the vacant apartment attached to the house. The husband would not let them deliver it. I called him up and gave him hell. Prior to settlement, I asked the seller if there were any defects in this house. He said, "Yes, the basement floods." Boy, did it flood. On New Year's Eve of 1950, he took me downstairs to show me the coal furnace, a "coke fire." He asked, "What do you think of the furnace?" I said, "It looks like it is on its last legs." I was correct. We put in a new gas furnace.

The sellers still had not moved out and we had given notice that we were vacating the Washington, D.C. apartment. Luckily, we reached a compromise. We purchased their Duncan Fife dining room furniture and agreed that they could stay two more weeks. And we gave them an additional seventy-five dollars. To this day, we are still using the dining room set at 2822 Fort Scott Drive. So, I guess you could say that the sale was amicable.

Among the many improvements needed were a new gas furnace, a new roof, and a new fence. Still, the bungalow served its purpose. When our second child, Bill, was born, we purchased an air conditioner from Jim. Then we found out we had to insulate each wall and ceiling in the one-and-a-half-story house to make it comfortable. To insulate the walls with rock wool in the entire house cost $750. I thought it was a fortune at that time.

There was a reason I was so taken by the Nineteenth Street bungalow. It reminded me of the house my dad built on North Lafayette Street in Greenville just before he died. I loved that house, but my mother had to rent it out to the superintendent of Gibsons. She received fifty dollars per month—a lot of money during the depression. At the time, I didn't realize that she was forced by economics to do this. We moved to a small house on South Lafayette Street near my Uncle George's house. He owned some land on a hollow and allowed me to raise sweet corn on it. A man by the name of Cooper, who chewed tobacco and disliked kids, owned a sway back horse and wagon. For some reason, he took a shine to me and said he wouldn't rent his horse to anyone but me. He called me Walk, a nickname which stuck with some.

One day I was driving the horse and wagon from South Lafayette Street to Mr. Cooper's house across from Uncle Will's Potato office. We were going down a small hill when the wagon hit the horse's legs. The horse broke into a gallop and the wagon began to weave back and forth across the pavement. I couldn't reign up the horse, so I drove the whole kit and caboodle over the curb into a large tree. That stopped the horse and wagon. Uncle George came along and helped me get back onto the street.

Chapter IX

The Power Company and the Purchase of 2822 Fort Scott Drive

We had a near disruption in the neighborhood in 1969. A real-estate man approached us about selling our house. By now, the solo law practice was doing very well, and we had purchased a three-unit apartment house at 618 Eighteenth Street. The real estate agent wanted to buy both properties. We were curious and asked who the buyer was. He said it was an out-of-town buyer, but wouldn't reveal the name.

I found out through the law office next door that the prospective buyer was actually the power company. Now, as we all know, a power company can exercise the right of eminent domain. Thinking that we would be forced to sell through court action or negotiation, we chose the latter and negotiated a price higher than the value of the property. An article appeared in the *Evening Star*, making the matter public. We believed we had done the neighborhood a good deed. Some people did not see it that way.

As far as I knew, the power company had a contract on just one other property. Their plan was to buy half the block and construct a substation. Of course, some of the owners in the half block wanted contracts. Apparently, others outside the half block threatened to file legal action. The power company backed off. Then, they sold the properties back to the owners and forfeited the difference between the actual value and the purchase price.

In retrospect, it was better for everybody involved and better for the neighborhood–we got to save the Nineteenth Street bungalow for posterity.

The substation was eventually built on vacant land one block away from the land owned by Cafritz. I have often thought that the power company used this move of buying houses as a feint, knowing that they would be opposed wherever they sought to build a substation: "Oh, you want us to build on vacant land? All right; we will build over there, and avoid a long and drawn-out fight."

It wasn't long before it became obvious that we needed a bigger house. With two teenage boys and a twelve-year-old girl, we simply didn't have enough bedrooms. We found a house made of antique brick and with a beautiful view at 2800 Grant Street in Aurora Hills. It had five bedrooms, three baths, nearly a quarter acre of land, and Fort Scott Park in the back. We were told the house already had a bid of $55,500 on it. Janet suggested that we offer $250 more, and the sellers accepted it. I put a mortgage on the Nineteenth Street house, which had been paid off, and used the money for a down payment. That gave us the leverage to assume the $15,000 mortgage, financed at 5.5 percent.

I'd made one tactical error, however. I thought that with the eminent domain threat, the capital gains from the forfeiture profit would not be taxed. I did some research, and concluded that full tax was due. I had to borrow $7,500 on an unsecured loan at a high rate of interest to pay the tax. I always advise my clients and my children: "If you want to be successful, pay your taxes." Taxes are necessary for governments to function. Of course, everyone wants to pay the tax that is legally due and no more, which is fine with the government.

I will continue with the history of the Nineteenth Street house. When we moved to 2800 South Grant Street, we had the house number changed to 2822 Fort Scott Drive because the driveway and front entrance faced Fort Scott. We had converted the duplex at 601 South Nineteenth Street to a single family house and kept it as a rental property for many years. We refinanced it in 1971 and used some of the cash out for a down payment on our farm near Skyline Drive. More about that later.

In 2000 we sold the Nineteenth Street house to Tom Fletcher, a young title attorney working across the hall for Jerry Williams. Tom did a brilliant job with it. We probably could have sold it for more, but we trusted Tom to preserve the integrity of the bungalow. The house had a great deal of sentimental value to us, as we there with from February of 1951 to August of 1969. I recommended that he tear off the apartment, which was not as well built as the main house, creating a buildable lot next to the main house. Unfortunately, it wasn't quite that easy. The lot required five thousand square feet with fifty feet of frontage, fifty feet in the back, and a 120 foot depth. Though the five thousand square foot requirement was more than met, the extra lot was ten inches short of the sixteen foot requirement between houses. This was due to a corner of the lot that was encroached by Fern Street.

Tom researched the title history of the property. He submitted a proposal to the county, which recommended building on the vacant lot and keeping the main house on the short lot.

At first, he was turned down flatly. He was told there was no way he could do this. But in his research, he'd found that Fern Street sliced off a part of the lot on which the main house stood. He appealed to a higher authority, stating that the main house had been on a full-fledged lot before Fern Street was developed and sliced off a corner of it; it was therefore "grandfathered." The appeal authority found that Tom was right. However, the new lot was still about ten inches short of the required sixteen feet between the main house and the new lot, as well as the fifty foot requirement. To solve this, Tom was required to apply for a variance before the Board of Zoning Appeals. They really put him through the hoops.

First, Tom knocked on every neighbor's door telling them what he proposed. He received no objection from the neighbors. Then, he called on me to come to the hearing and speak in favor of the variance. He said zoning attorneys' fees are high. The night of the hearing, there were only three members present out of a total of five. One board member was African-American. In my presentation, I focused on the value of preserving the history of the house and its sentimental value. We didn't want to see it torn down. In conclusion, I said, "I think it is reasonable to grant the variance." The African-American member jumped to his feet and said, "It is more than reasonable; I move that we grant the variance." The motion was passed unanimously.

Tom put in three new bathrooms, a bedroom upstairs, new kitchen, new siding, and new roof. He says it is a Sears, Roebuck and Co. bungalow—very much in demand in Arlington. I told him and his wife that I hoped they made a lot of money from the property. They have four children deserving to prosper.

A town house in Vienna's Country Creek neighborhood caught my eye and I did an IRS 10-31 tax exchange with the proceeds from the Nineteenth Street house. My good friend Ike Seekford was our buyer's agent. Located near the Vienna Metro stop, the Country Creek community was strikingly well kept due to the very fussy Homeowners Association! We cooperated with the HOA in every way we can.

Before we left 601, we talked about the move from Nineteenth Street to 2822 Fort Scott Drive. Today, June 29, 2006, I am writing on that dining room table in 2822. We have enjoyed this house; I love this house more than the Greenville bungalow. It is a place for my beloved daughter, Elaine to come to when she gets a break from her job as a Physician's Assistant in North Carolina. The view is not as good as it was when we bought it; Crystal City high-rise buildings have crept in over the years. We are now the oldest residents in the immediate neighborhood. The house has needed some repairs because of the loam of the soil, which caused cracks in split foyer's lower level. However, by watering around the foundation, creating a slope, running tile from the downspouts away from the house, and installing shields to prevent leaves and debris from getting into the gutters, the water now runs over gutters. We have been able to keep the cracks at bay. Mr. Breeden, one of my close neighbors, told their buyer that we were the best neighbors they've ever had.

Chapter X

The Shinns, Real Estate

I have to tell you about the Shinns, who lived in a duplex next to us at Nineteenth Street. Captain Shinn was the naval attaché for South Korea. They had three boys and Janet taught Mrs. Shinn English. The boys picked up English right away from their teachers and classmates at Nellie Custis Elementary School. We got along famously, but there were times when East met West, and nary the 'twain would meet!

One evening, Mrs. Shinn said to me, "Mr. Walker is always home at night. Why don't you go to Geisha house?"

Janet said, "We do not have Geisha houses in America."

Captain Shinn said, "When my boys marry, then I will have daughters."

Later, we had a visit from one of the grown boys. He had the cutest little Korean girl. Later, one of the boys visited us at this house—he was a graduate student at the University of Wisconsin. Mrs. Shinn came all the way from South Korea to be here. We were having breakfast. I went out to pour some coffee for Janet and Mrs. Shinn. Mrs. Shinn said, "Mr. Walker, always the good husband." Of course, in Korea the men at that time did not do much around the house.

We have not heard from them as of late.

I am going to relate to you our real-estate purchases, in chronological order, all of which turned out well. My hope is that you can glean some good investment ideas from our experiences and use them to make some successful purchases of your own. They did not happen overnite but over a lifetime.

First, I believe real estate is the best investment, though there are flat periods. As one real estate investor said about taking a home equity to invest in the stock market, "You might as well go to Las Vegas."

Also, don't forget the old cliché, "Location, location, location." The stock market is somewhat of a gamble. However, money can be made there. I have one of my IRAs with Fidelity. Overall, the stock market has done well for us.

First, there was 601 Nineteenth Street. We sold it for twenty-one times what we paid for it. Here's an interesting example illustrating how real estate values change. Mr. Nagle, who once pastured cows on the land where the Nineteenth Street house stands, came by one day while I was working on the porch. He said, "Boy, you really got taken on this property. It only cost four thousand to build." Of course, that was back in 1926. We paid $12,600 in 1951. I said respectfully to Mr. Nagle, "Prices for real estate change over the years."

After we sold the Nineteenth Street house, another real-estate agent told me he thought the *buyer* certainly made out. Well, I wanted the buyer to make out. Furthermore, Tom Fletcher did exactly what we'd hoped: He preserved the bungalow for posterity. We did a 10-31 exchange on the sale of 601. At first, Tom's wife believed we owed a fee to the property manager. I explained that a three percent fee to the property manager was due only if the property was sold to the tenant. I wanted Tom and his family to make out. We had made enough.

The next purchase was a duplex on Uhle Street near Glebe Road. These small, well-built units have two bedrooms. I recall that we paid $9,500 in 1959. Janet was not too keen about it. However, I intended to build equity and create income. I sold it myself to a carpenter in 1962. He financed it with a second trust, which we held. What we did with the three-thousand-dollar check amazes me to this day, and may amaze you, too. I had a vision of grandeur—a plan to build a small office building. However, the same year, a house on the corner of Barton Street, came up for sale. The asking price was forty-four thousand dollar. I was interested. This property was owned by a large group of heirs.

One day the executrix came into my office and said, "You can have the property for $27,500 if you buy it right now." I said, "Well, give us time to get a contract."

I went to the First Virginia Bank to get a loan. The loan officer for First Virginia Bank said, "Why, this is the Golden Triangle," a bevy of old houses located between the Court House and Sears in Arlington. He said, "I will go in on it with you." I thought, who could be a better partner than a bank mortgage officer? He secured a first trust from the United Savings and Loan for $22,500 to avoid a conflict.

Then, just two weeks later he said, "Woody, I'm leaving the bank to go into the building business." My heart leapt into my throat. I said, "Jerry, I would think long and hard before I left the security of the bank to go into such an unsure business." He left. I probably don't need to tell you what happened to his building business—Jerry did not go into bankruptcy, and he paid off all the debt. I took care of everything on the Barton property: finding tenants and property managers, and paying bills and taxes. Janet was concerned that I was doing more than my share of the work, but by doing it myself, I said that is all right—I knew it was being done right. I was very honest about receipts and expenditures. I kept meticulous records. And every time I asked Jerry for funds, he came up with the money. He trusted me implicitly. We sold the Barton Street house under an assemblage in 1988—something that probably had never been done, or on such a scale that I know of in this country. I will tell you about that later.

Out next property purchase took place in 1967. It was a three-unit apartment house at 618 Eighteenth Street in Arlington. It was on the same block as our first bungalow. After settlement, we rode back to the courthouse with the sellers, who asked, "What do you know that we don't?" Of course, we knew nothing and I said so, other than we thought it was a good real estate investment.

One of our shared dreams was to buy a farm. The search was full of disappointments. One that I particularly remember was in Sperryville, Virginia. It was advertised as a bungalow. I had visions of President Hoovers' cabin, fly fishing, etc. The young man took us through weeds up to your shoulders to a vacant structure. It was an old chicken house with no windows and I asked, "Is this the bungalow?" He said, "Yes." We said, "goodbye." I would not put chickens in that structure. Well, we had many other disappointments, but first, this tale about the unhappy sale of the three-unit apartment house.

We bought the Eighteenth Street apartment house in 1967. Our three children, Jon, Bill, Elaine, and my wife, Janet hated the place. They said I spent too much time there even though I had a property manager. Of course, we were responsible for all the upkeep, inside and out. We sold it through a local real-estate agent in 1971. The buyers were a group who expected a zoning change in the neighborhood, which never happened. However, they made out by fixing up the houses and selling them for a profit. After the settlement was completed, the agent said to me, "I am not looking out for your interests." I thought, *Well, thank you very much—I am paying your six percent commission.* As an attorney, I always put the interests of my client ahead of everything else. For this sale, we took back a ten-thousand-dollar second trust, which was paid like clockwork by an advertising manager of *The Washington Post.*

Here's what we did with this second trust. Prior to August 1971, Elaine became horse-conscious. This was at about the same time that we became serious about buying a family farm. She had been taking riding lessons at the same place President Ford's daughter took lessons, and we were looking to purchase a horse for her. I said, "If this stable is good enough for President Ford's daughter, then it is good enough for my daughter." We found a fine chestnut horse by the name of Gypsy. Gypsy was half-Arabian and half-quarter horse. I said, "Elaine, where are we going to put the horse—in Fort Scott Park?" Of course, Arlington did not permit horses—except at Fort Myer.

Gypsy was a show horse owned by a Loudoun County family. The daughter in the family was going to college and they needed money for tuition. Gypsy cost three hundred dollars. The family agreed to board the horse for a fee until we found a place of our own.

The search for a farm resumed when we came across an advertisement that a veterinarian had a lighted barn and house for sale in Green County. Getting there was quite a long trip down Sky Line drive. Again, I pictured a nice barn; certainly a veterinarian would have a nice barn with electricity. Guess what the barn looked like? Four posts for a rough roof with a bare bulb hanging down. The South River ran near the house, which was nice, but it was beside a derelict old house, which needed to be torn down. The South River looked beautiful on the nice sunny afternoon and was four to five feet deep. The only problem was that we could see that during hurricane weather the river would surely flood "the lighted barn." The kids liked the river and the house. I said, "It's too far away, and there were too many other negatives." So much for the lighted barn.

We looked at another farm in Orange County, which had a huge lake on its property. We were not interested in a huge lake.

We had many disappointments in our search for a farm.

In August of 1971, we took Elaine to see Luray Caverns. A colleague and friend from American Law Division, Charles Wood (who ran for Arlington County Board and was now in Front Royal) recommended that we visit Arthur Vaughn, a leading real-estate man in Front Royal. We did, and we never made it to the caverns. We looked at some acreage near the Shenandoah Park on old abandoned Route 622, where we committed to buy approximately twenty acres. Later, Mr. Vaughn called in regard to a farm for sale. I talked to Billy Vaughn, Arthur's son. He said the price was $750 per acre. I asked if he would entertain an offer. He said no. I knew the state assessor and gave him a call, telling him how much the land cost. He said, "That is kind of high." I said, "But it has black walnut trees." He said, "Then it is worth it." The walnut trees have now been cut, and that is a story in itself that I will tell you about later.

Shortly thereafter, I stopped in again to see Mr. Vaughn. He took me for a ride down Browntown road, then left onto 622 and up a sloping field to Sky Line Drive. Right then and there I told him I would take everything on that side of the road, leading up to the park. We went back to his office and I signed papers and gave him another thousand-dollar down payment. It turned out to be the best investment we ever made as I will reveal to you later. At this time, I wasn't buying for investment, but for a place to put my daughter's horse, and a family farm.

I told Mr. Vaughn, a very sharp but easy-to-deal-with businessman, "I want a survey." Mr. Vaughn said, "Mr. Walker, we don't do surveys down here." I said, "Mr. Vaughn, that is the way I do it." The survey revealed that he had more acreage than he thought. From our point of view, and in retrospect, it was a very good move to buy just on one side of Route 622. It would have been awkward to have the horses and cattle across the road. In the end, we'd purchased seventy-two plus acres, an old barn, a wood shed, a spring house, a branch of Lands Run, and two pond sites.

We put my daughter's horse on the farm in the spring of 1972. We didn't settle until June of 1972 at Mr. Vaughn's request. Mr. Vaughn offered a land contract, but I wanted a deed and a deed of trust. However, I'm sure Mr. Vaughn would have delivered a marketable title at the end of a land contract. Possible judgment liens and other liens are the primary reasons an owner is unable to deliver a marketable title under a land contract.

From this lawyer's point of view, it is not a good idea to buy land under a land contract. Amen. My cousin Lloyd Walker, longtime Mayor of Greenville, said that some lawyers believe it is a perfectly legitimate way to transfer land, but I disagree.

We also purchased from Reamy a 3.7 acre lot next to our farm. We did this to prevent anyone else from building next our farm, and to prevent hunting.

Mr. Reamy wanted to hold the lot. To my knowledge, Mrs. Reamy never came down to look at the lot and did want to sell. Mr. Vaughn had the lot listed for sale. The listing had run out.

I asked Mr. Vaughn if he had any objection to our making a direct purchase. Mr. Vaughn said he had no objection as long as another realtor was not involved. We made a cash offer to the Reamys, substantially above what they had paid the Lenderkings. Mr. Reamy said, "I don't know whether we want to sell." If you ever saw a wife shoot daggers at her husband, it was Mrs. Reamy. Of course, Mr. Reamy sold the lot. The Mrs. did not want to live down there.

In 1990 my beloved wife, Janet picked out a cedar ranch-style house plan to be built on the farm. I said I was not going to build a house until we had paid for the land. Bill had built a room on the second floor of the barn. Ray Smelser said that the room served its purpose. It was paneled and had a polished beam. However, there was a lot of weight up there supported by posts. Leroy Compton put in wood supports—I added steel posts. It seems to be holding as long as Bill doesn't put anything more up there. Bill is now building a machine shop on the farm.

The plan for the ranch house included a large kitchen, two bedrooms, a living room, a bathroom with a tub and shower—and we now had running water and a commode. We no longer had to use the ladies bathrooms, named the "Devil's Rock" by a previous owner.

Bill suggested we add two feet to the side of both bedrooms. We also added a six-foot screened porch on the front. You will notice in the photo that we have added a flag pole and we fly "Old Glory" with the Virginia flag beneath.

Our next real estate purchase didn't take place until 1994. We were driving down Liberty Hall Road when Janet and I noticed a Weichert Realty sign in front of what we called "the doctor's property." We stopped at the Weichert Realty office in Front Royal that Sunday night. I told the lady I would make an offer equal to what we paid for the timber on our farm. I thought it was odd that she did not get out a contract.

I took the name of the listing agent from the sign. Now get this—how fast this goes. That same evening, I told the lady in Vienna, "We will make you an offer: we offer the same amount of money that we paid for our timber land."

The lady said, "Mr. Walker, we have already received two offers higher than your offer."

I said, "All right, I will just pay your price." She gave something of a sigh, and I asked, "What's the matter?" She said, "We wanted it." I said, "Be in my office tomorrow morning and I will give you ten thousand dollars cash as a down payment on the contract." The price was $135,000.

The real-estate agent was in our office promptly the next morning, despite getting lost in Rosslyn. The contract signed was for sixty acres, more or less. I got the survey later (violating my policy of getting a survey before settlement) because I sensed that there was a great deal of interest in the property. Time was of the essence. Indeed, there were two back-up contracts at the settlement.

The real-estate agent told me that there were two back-up contracts, and told them that Mr. Walker had a firm contract. They said, "We are putting in the contracts in case Mr. Walker fails." I said, "Mr. Walker is not going to fail." We got a survey later which revealed the area to be sixty-four acres.

We also got Chicago Title Insurance on the property. We paid cash. Here's how we did it—we sold the Calvert lots and had paid the capital gains taxes earlier. A 10-31 property-exchange tax attorney told us we could back-date the contract—I said, "I would not do that, and I will pay the tax."

We took a first trust on the Fort Scott Drive house for one-hundred-thousand dollars at six percent interest with no penalty for extra principal payments or early payoff. As I recall, we paid off that mortgage in two years. One of my attorney friends asked, "Woody, don't you know you can be land poor?" I said, "Yes, but we will recoup on the timber." Little did he know, or did we know how valuable the timber was and that this land would become.

Unbeknown to us, the timing was excellent on our sixty-four-acre purchase. Indeed, it was full of huge tulip poplars, red oaks, white oaks, and ash.

At that time, ash brought the highest price. We timbered forty acres in a forestry manner, cutting down only to nineteen inches in the back of the property. The timber cruiser said the contract was the best that he'd heard of.

Now there were also four cinder-block cabins on the property. The Doctors had used them as summer getaways. They were well constructed, with steel roofs. At first, we didn't know what to do with these cabins. One had been Dr. Watt's cabin. He gave the property to the Medical College of the City of New York—for this, they named a professor's chair after him.

While going through the Dr. Watt's cabin we found his daughter's wedding pictures, his graduation book from Davidson College, and some medical books. I found that Dr. Watt was in Norfolk, and called him long distance. Dr. Watt answered gruffly, "What do you want?" Now, Dr. Watt was, I understood, eighty-seven years old.

I said, "Dr. Watt, I do not want anything, but I believe that we have something you want." I told him what we'd found.

Dr. Watt said, "If you would send those articles to me, I would be ever grateful to you." We sent them down to Dr. Watt and he sent a very nice note to us saying he was glad we had bought the land, and that if he were there, he would have helped us obtain it because we had a greater love of the land than he had.

To continue the saga of this property, the surveyor said, "You'd better get those cabins surveyed or they will change the rules on you." He was so right. I told him we didn't want to go before the Planning Commission—we would do it administratively if possible. He got the four cabin lots perked for three bedrooms and wells. It amounted to about eleven acres including the private access road. The lots with approvals and restrictions were recorded on the land records in Warren County.

Now, there was a reaction by a small number of people on Liberty Hall Road. I was told that nine owners were involved in creating a petition without our knowledge, which did not make us very happy. The leader was a newcomer. Because we were unaware of the petition, we did not attend the hearing. We were told that Mr. Stanley, the Warren County Manager, told the petitioners, "This is a done deal." The petition and hearing were wasted time and energy. We had been farmers on the road since 1973, and became then, and still are, the largest landowners, with 128 acres on the road. We don't intend to sell any more land.

But we did sell the four cabin lots to Whittington, who lived on the road. He said he wanted the five-acre parcel for his son and the three-acre parcel for his brother. I thought there could be no better buyer than Whittington: He was a neighbor on the road, and selling all four cabins and parcels to one buyer was wise. We would need the income from the sale later, as you will see.

Our latest real-estate purchase took place in November of 2006, if you can call it that. We paid cash, eighteen thousand dollars, for six cemetery lots at Columbia Gardens in Arlington. A number of my friends from American Law Division and private practice are buried around our plots. Janet and I are eligible to be buried in Arlington National Cemetery, as I am a veteran; however, I want to be buried with my children.

I don't think at this late stage we will buy any more real estate.

Chapter XI

Law Practice

We had a very successful and interesting law practice. My friends said that leaving a secure job as a government attorney on Capitol Hill with three children and a mortgage took a lot of courage.

My sister asked, "How are you going to feed your family?"

A local delegate to the Virginia General Assembly told me, "Woodrow, it is virtually impossible to start a solo-law practice in a major metropolitan area." However, he qualified it with, "unless you are in the channel of trade." You will see later that his words were prophetic. I will say this: It will scare the hell out of you.

My chief of staff of the Fortieth Infantry Division, George Latimer, was on the Military Court of Appeals here in Washington. I was granted an appointment with him upon leaving the American Law Division. I believe he was one of the defense attorneys for Lieutenant Calley. In regard to law practice he said, "The practice of law will kill you."

You will recall that I tried unsuccessfully to transfer out of Headquarters Fortieth Infantry to the Air Force. At that time he said, "We trained this man and he is going to stay right here." I knew then that that was where I was going to be. My Uncle HN said when I was assigned to the Fortieth HQ, "you are well placed." He was so right.

However, I received a lot of encouragement to go into private practice from Dr. Freeman Sharp in the American Law Division. The chief of the divison, Mr. Gilbert, said up on my leaving, "Woodrow, you have got it right in you. You will do just fine."

I was admitted to the Virginia State Bar on motion without question. We had just bought a semi-detached house in Arma Valley, which we had previously rented. Again, I had saved some money, had some stocks, and we had the apartment next to the house with a separate entrance. I cashed in my retirement from the American Law Division and used it as start-up money.

I rented one room close to the courthouse in the insurance building, which already had a number of attorneys as tenants. This location put me in the legal channel of trade. This proved to be helpful. I am going to have to give credit to some older attorneys who willingly helped me succeed. First, Tony Sicillano. He stated that Lyon Tyler was looking for a Virginia attorney to handle his Virginia business. He was in the Investment Building on the comer of K and Fifteenth Streets in Washington, D.C. I could write a book on Lyon Tyler. He was a former FBI agent in espionage and had gone into practice with a colleague from the bureau. Lyon was a great guy and I enjoyed working with him.

I also had the opportunity to buy all of John Daly's law books and furniture. He was one of Tony's partners and was located in the Investment Building in Washinton, D.C. I do not know why he sold his Virginia books and furniture. George Grove had left almost the entire Virginia reports—which I used—in a book case behind my desk. All of John Daly's stuff—a secretary's walnut desk, his books, etc.—were of very high quality.

I was all set up and ready for law practice.

Speaking of established attorneys who sent me cases (which were probably tough cases they didn't want), I want to mention Lee Bean. Lee suffered from polio and was handicapped. But that didn't slow him down. Lee did more civic work than most of us without a disability. He said, "There is no better young attorney on the Square than Woodrow Walker." However, I was not all that young at the time. I can't write about many of my cases, but I will single out a few that I think you might find interesting. We handled a lot of routine commercial cases, as many as twenty-five in one court appearance.

In my first year in practice, 1960, Tyler woke me in the middle of the night. He said that we had to go to Prince William Court and get the CIC Investment Co. boys out of jail. They had repossessed a car and were in jail because there was a claim that they had stolen tools that had been left in the car. Of course, the young men had no intent to steal those tools, nor to take permanent dominion over them. The procedure was to take the tools out of the car and leave them at Jim McKay's Chevrolet in Fairfax, so the buyer could pick them up.

We had a meeting with the Commonwealth Attorney of Prince William County. We argued the "no intent" theory. The Commonwealth attorney stated that it was his duty as the Commonwealth attorney to protect the innocent as well as to punish the guilty, and with that said, he said, "I am going to drop the case." At that moment, Tyler's lighter flashed and played "Dixie." I accused him of setting it off on purpose. He claimed he had not.

Now, the repossessed car owner's son had filed the complaint. Tyler recommended we settle with him. I disagreed—I asked, "Why settle? He is wrong." Tyler said, "Better to take your licking early." I talked with the owner of the vehicle—he had just returned home from deer hunting. As I recall, the car was in the street. So, the repossessors had the legal right to take the car. He said, "If I had found them taking my car, I would have shot them." I believe he was telling the truth.

It is my opinion that one doesn't own a car until it is paid for. Until then, the bank or financing company owns the car with you. If you do not think so, get behind in your car payments.

Another interesting case from that first year involved a client who received a reckless-driving charge. He was found guilty of not stopping for a school bus on the other side of a median strip.

Route 50 has a median strip and multiple lanes. At the time, the speed limit was high—fifty-five miles per hour—and stopping created a traffic hazard because overtaking cars could not stop. An amendment to the law that exempted this type of highway would not endanger school children, simply because they do not cross the highway when unloading. I contacted my friend, delegate Harrison Mann. He told me to send a letter. I did, and the law was changed. This shows how one citizen can make a difference.

First Accident Case
Another case, this one in February of 1960, was a contested accident case. I won the case with help from my witness, a solid citizen from Manassas. After the hearing, the defendant walked out of the courtroom saying, "Now you got a judgment, let's see you collect!"

He was right. He was judgment-proof.

We got around it though, by sending the judgment to the Department of Motor Vehicles. Now, the defendant couldn't get a license until the judgment was paid. About two years later, he had married. The little woman called and asked, "Would you write to the DMV to suspend the prohibition of the judgment if we made payments?"

I said, "Certainly!" The payments were made like clockwork.

The first year of law practice was kind of skinny—we grossed three thousand dollars. The next year was better, and I knew I had chosen the right field. By 1963, I had earned an annual salary of seven thousand dollars, the same as when I left the American Law Division. Don't forget that we had other income. The family didn't miss any meals. And after 1960 vacations, nor did we miss any mortgage payments. Now, seven thousand dollars seems like a small amount, but it was good money in the early 1960s.

Fort Myer Embezzlement Case

Another case you may find interesting involved two young men, both nine-teen years old. They worked for the government at Fort Myer. One day, the manager entrusted them to courier approximately seven thousand dollars to the bank. The boys cooked up a scheme in which one would hit the other over the head, and report a robbery. When it came time for one of the boys to hit the other, he couldn't do it. Instead, they just took the money bag to their living quarters. My recollection is that the FBI was there in 30 minutes, and confiscated all of the money.

This was an appointed Federal case in Alexandria, and not the first one I had been offered. I had declined a draft-dodger case because as a war vet-eran, my heart would not be with the defense. The next case I was offered involved an attempt on President Nixon's life. Because of a conflict I ended up with the embezzlement case. I understand that the Nixon case went to the Supreme Court of the United States.

I appeared at the preliminary hearing of the embezzlement case with a motion to dismiss. The magistrate, King, was irritated, wanting to know on what grounds. "My grounds, sir, are that the prosecution has not cited the federal statute that will serve as the basis for this case." The motion shook up the prosecution and the FBI. The FBI witness for the prosecution said, "Mr. Walker, we will get that information to you right away."

The other attorney, Mr. Young, and I appeared at the hearing before Federal Judge Oren Lewis. Sullivan, the probation officer, said, "He [the judge] is in a bad mood. He is not going to give them probation. They're going up the river." It was a dreary, Monday rainy day. I represented the Filipino boy whose dad was a master sergeant in the Filipino Scouts. I talked for thirty minutes before Judge Lewis—my argument ran off him like water off a duck's back. I could see that I was making no headway. My stomach was churning because I really thought they were going to jail. I finally said, "Judge, I have investigated this case—both of these boys are good workers." Magic words!

The judge turned to Sullivan and asked, "Mr. Sullivan, can you get these boys a job?" Mr. Sullivan responded, "Yes, sir." "All right," Judge Lewis said, "I am going to give them probation. If they are ever before me again, they will get the maximum." What a result. My client never got into serious trou-ble, but I did get him a divorce. He got a job driving a mail truck.

I firmly believe that this result was far better than sending a young man to a federal penitentiary, where he most certainly would have learned to become a hardened criminal. Think of the financial cost to society. Think of saving a young life. I was paid five hundred dollars for the representation—a reasonable attorney fee at the time.

Jury Trial Case—Claim Lien Paid Off

Another early case involved an auto repossessed by the finance company. The defendant had stolen the car back. The company had made an error, marking the lien as paid, when in fact he hadn't paid a dime. The defendant insisted he had paid the lien in cash. He was given a jury trial in the Arlington County Circuit Court by Judge Hosmer. The company had cash register receipts showing that there had been no such transaction, as well as the testimony of the cashier clerk. The financial manager thought I was too meticulous—he accused me of beating a dead horse. However, the deputy sheriff for the Arlington Circuit Court told me that he had seen the defendant beat this type of case in the past. The jury came back in after about thirty minutes with a verdict for the plaintiff. The best part of the story is that the defendant went down to the bank the next day—took out a second trust and paid the balance, thus proving that he owed the money.

Tyler had a number of Virginia attorneys. He said I had done the best of any of them. It looked like again I was in the right jobs: private law practice and agriculture. I loved both of these pursuits.

Extortion Case

A case that made the Washington Post involved two deaf boys. One boy was husky, the other small. The boys were charged with extortion because they had threatened another individual at his home. The small lad's cousin from West Virginia called me and asked to join their defense because he wanted the experience of practicing law in the big city.

I said, "I'll take all the help I can get." The Commonwealth Attorney's Office took a hard tack and moved ahead with prosecution. When the small defendant testified, the judge called us into chambers and asked if a settlement could be reached. It could not. The judge stated there was enough evidence to bind them over.

However, the Commonwealth dropped the case before it got to Circuit Court. After that, I received a Christmas card from the smaller boy's mother every year until her recent death.

I had a general law practice and I handled the defense for a number of early criminal cases. Early in practice, the Assistant Commonwealth Attorney in Fairfax said in a tampering case, "Your boy is going to jail for thirty days." I said, "Let's see what the judge says." None of my clients was ever sentenced to a day behind bars, a pretty good record. This young man served a weekend in jail by the consent of his parents and the defendant; and at the suggestion of the judge. The charge of tampering was then dismissed. Other cases concerned commercial, personal-injury, divorce, bankruptcy, wills, and estate matters.

I also represented a major bank, a major national retailer, a major finance company, and a new old line car dealership in Arlington for which I never lost a case. You can see our law practice was in the channel of trade. We also represented our clients in defense and as bankruptcy creditors. We also represented them in numerous commercial and collection matters.

Slip and Fall Case
In 1989, I represented a returning client in a slip-and-fall case. Everything I did for this client turned out well. He was quite a heavy man. During a three-day ice storm, he returned to his home in Fairlington; slipped on the ice; fell; and broke his shoulder, which later deteriorated into a frozen shoulder.

The adjustor and I hit it off immediately. He was an ex-marine sergeant, I a veteran Army sergeant from World War II. We settled the case for approximately eighty-nine thousand dollars. It was said to be one of the largest slip-and-fall recoveries in Northern Virginia at that time. My client elected to take a structured settlement, which paid him a fixed amount over fifteen years. The payment would come from a small insurance company. I asked, "Suppose this insurance company goes into bankruptcy?" He said, "Our company State Farm will guarantee it." I said, "Put it in writing."

He did, and the small insurance company did go kaput. I won't bore you with the details of the case. I did do a very good job of presenting the case to the insurance company. The doctor was also very good.

Drug Case
The next case I am going to tell you about is a serious drug case involving a cocaine sale. My client was a young man, nineteen years old. The violation occurred in Arlington County. He was arrested in South Carolina, when I was hired by his grandmother, for whom every case on which I worked turned out well. The young man had minor traffic offenses, which I had previously represented. So I knew he had a temper. His South-Carolina attorney and I recommended that he agree to extradition, and he did.

Knowing his quick temper, I told him, "It is going to be 'Yes, sir', and 'No sir', all the way back in the plane with the Arlington detective." He obeyed. I talked with the Arlington Commonwealth attorney Henry Hudson, now a federal judge in the Eastern District of the United States (and judge in the Vick dog fighting case). I proposed a continuance of one year: If there were no further incidents, the case would be dismissed.

He said, "I cannot agree with that, but I will not oppose it." The boy's family was present in force and well dressed, including his grandmother. The young man also spoke on his own behalf. The detective spoke in his favor and I made my motion.

Then it was Judge Duff's turn. He said, "All right, I am impressed with the presentation of counsel. I am impressed with the young man. I am going to grant the motion. However, every three months, he must send me a progress report and a copy of which to his counsel." The young man got a job in keeping with the judge's order. After that, I would occasionally see Judge Duff in the court house. He would ask, "Woody, did you get a copy of the young man's letter?" Of course I did. He had some minor trouble in South Carolina, but in the end, the case was dismissed.

Again, this was a far better result for the young man, his family, and his community: to be a productive member of society rather than going to the penitentiary. Even after the cases were over, I would work to help these young people to stay on the right track. They listened to me like I was an oracle. It seemed, however, that I didn't have the same effect on my own children, Jon, Bill, and Elaine at that time. What I tried to teach them did come back later, though.

Custody Case
Would you believe there was another highly-successful case for the grandmother? Remember, I said every case I took for this grandmother turned out well.

One of her sons was constantly getting into trouble. Someone had shot and killed his father. The same guy shot and killed the son. He got off in both cases; he got away with murder twice. The son married a girl who was voluptuous. One time he told me he came home and she was on the couch making out with his best friend.

A Montgomery County, Maryland detective called me stating that two small children of the son had been abandoned by the mother and asked if the grandmother would take custody. The grandmother had a good job with the power company. She said she would take the two children and care for them.

The grandmother asked for a court order, believing that the mother would pursue custody in order to collect social security. We got the uncontested court order. The mother filed suit in the Fairfax Juvenile and Domestic Relations Court, attempting to claim her first right to custody on the grounds that she was the mother. Normally, this is the way the case would go, and she hired a tough, veteran Fairfax attorney to represent her.

We went to a full-blown trial. The Fairfax attorney had stacks of case laws showing that the mother was entitled to custody. I had no case law; I had the Montgomery detective. The detective testified about the condition of the two children when they had been found abandoned.

The mother took the stand. She testified about plans to move into a new townhouse for the children. If my memory serves me correctly, she did not have much at that time. She did have a new, young mate. The one poignant question I asked her during cross-examination was, "Why, at this late date, are you so interested in custody? Is it social security?"

She rose from the stand à la Perry Mason and screamed, "I love my children! I am not interested in Social Security!" I rested my case.

The judge took the kids into another room and asked them with whom they wanted to live. The grandmother testified that the children were afraid of their mother. One can only imagine what Judge Jamborsky heard in his chambers.

The judge ruled that custody was to remain with the grandmother and that the mother was to have no visitation rights. Her veteran attorney was shocked—"You mean to say that the mother is to have no visitation rights?" The judge said, "That's right." The veteran attorney said, "We note an appeal."

Before the appeal had been perfected, I hired the Woody Clements Detective Agency to investigate the mother and her mate. They must have gotten wind of it because they dropped the appeal. Woody Clements later became the long-time Arlington sheriff. The grandmother raised the children. She deserves an award for the years she spent raising and protecting her grandchildren.

Fairfax Hospital Case

We did our share of pro bono work. Janet and I did a little public service that needs to be mentioned because it illustrated a strange case against smoking. A gentleman and his wife came into the office to do wills.—They could not make up their minds about what to do with their worldly goods upon death. He had to be admitted to Fairfax Hospital because he suffered from emphysema. Still, he couldn't make a decision to sign.

His brother, a prominent newspaper man for *The Washington Post*, called to ask about the results of the will.

"Of course he could not make up his mind."

He said, "I'll talk to him." We were summoned to the hospital that evening. We had prepared the will as directed. When it came time to sign the will, we discovered he could not sign his name. I told him to make an X in the appropriate place. Two nurses witnessed the signature. Janet notarized the documents. The will stood up, and he died shortly later from the emphysema.

I quit smoking thirty-nine years ago. However, if I had been a smoker when I witnessed the situation at the Fairfax Hospital that night, I would have quit tout de suite. When he couldn't sign his name, I had to walk out of the room.

Creditor Bankruptcy Cases and the *Washington Post* Photo

The *Washington Post* photo is connected to a large number of US bankruptcy cases in Alexandria. Among them was a trustee hearing in which I represented a large retailer.

It was Monday morning, and there had been a terrific storm over the weekend. We had been at the farm during the storm. I'd walked the fence line during the thunder and lightning—taking my life in my hands—to fix the fence.

The next morning I came in on the wrong side of town, and saw a police officer diverting traffic because Alexandria had flooded. I looked at the flooded streets—they didn't look much worse than what we had seen at the farm. I took off my shoes, rolled up my pant legs and started walking through the water. A store owner said, "Watch out for the curb." The water came up to my knees. I determined that if it got any higher, I would go back. It did not. I stopped at one place and was interviewed by a TV man who asked where I was going.

I said, "I'm going to a US Bankruptcy Trustees hearing," and proceeded down Union Street barefooted as you can see in the photo. Unbeknown to me, a *Washington Post* photographer took my picture. I was putting on my shoes at the hearing-room entrance when he approached me and asked my name. Who would've guessed that this picture would end up on the front page of *The Post*?

At 7:00 A.M. the next morning, my son Bill called me to say, "Dad, you made the front page of the *Washington Post*."

I said, "You have got to be kidding." It was a large picture, occupying the top left quarter of the front page. *The Post* reporter got it a little wrong—the caption said I was a US trustee in bankruptcy, which I was not (it was corrected the next day). However, ninety-nine percent of the Bar members in northern Virginia thought it was great, and my dedication was good publicity for the bars. The photo was posted in the clerk's office of the Alexandria District Court for two years and two months with the caption, "Lawyer of the Month."

Of course, there is always a little professional jealousy in every career field. It's human nature. Soon afterward I received a little ribbing while at the Prince William General District Court office. One lawyer said, "Woody, you ought to make them take down that picture in the Alexandria clerk's office."

Another young lawyer quietly responded, "What do you mean? It's a Norman Rockwell picture."

The same morning that my son Bill called, the executive secretary of the Arlington Bar, Betty Waldo, came over to the office and said, "This is only the second time that a member's picture of the Arlington County Bar has been on the front page of *The Post*." The other time was in 1941, when a group of the Arlington Bar golfers won a trophy at the Washington Golf and Country Club. Betty also said, "I think it is just great."

The next day I was in Loudoun General District Court. Judge Cannon said, "Mr. Walker, I enjoyed the picture." One attorney said, "Woody, this is your fifteen minutes of fame."

Hope Diggs of Alexandria District Court said, "You are a celebrity." One of the bankruptcy attorney's office secretaries offered, "What good-looking legs, what a guy!" The photo is hanging in our office.

Upon my retirement from practicing law, Martindale-Hubbell had given me, for a number of years, the highest rating preeminent attorney.

The Korean Case

When I first joined the Arlington County Bar Association, African Americans were not admitted. There came a time to vote on this matter. I believe it was Tom Monroe who applied first. I voted to admit Tom Monroe. He won and was admitted.

He was later appointed with Bar recommendation to be a district court judge in Arlington.

I had a number of cases before this very good judge (who later became a circuit court judge). One contested criminal case stands out: an elderly Korean man who was charged with hit and run.

I had this man come into the office on a Saturday morning. Grilling him, I told him I thought he would lose. The Assistant Commonwealth Attorney was Art Karp, an excellent and experienced prosecutor.

He had an array of witnesses; all I had was the old Korean and his daughter. The Korean insisted he was not driving this car.

With not much testimony from my two witnesses, I arose to summarize by stating that I had this man in my office Saturday morning grilling him, and he emphatically denied being in the car. Despite of all the testimony of all the witnesses for the prosecution, not one witness put the defendant in the car.

After weighing the evidence of both sides, Judge Monroe said: "When a man emphatically denies he was in the car it creates doubt of his guilt: case dismissed."

Chapter XII

Civic Activities

Throughout my career, I have been engaged in a number of civic activities, including being vice president of the Arlington Utilities Commission, where we helped to secure the admittance of the Red Top Cab Company as a business in the county. I also served as president and counsel of the Calvary Foundation; and president of the Nellie Custis PTA, for which I helped raise $350,000 to pay for building additions and a kindergarten.

I was vice president of Jefferson Civic Association, and helped get the county to purchase the land for Fort Scott Park and Virginia Highlands Park.

I also held a number of other offices in Calvary Methodist Church and was president of the Betchler Class and superintendent of the Adult Education as well as the registered agent of the Foundation.

I mentioned earlier that one of my civic endeavors involved the Red Top Cab Company, which is now a thriving business in Arlington County. While I was doing civic work on the Arlington County Public Utilities Commission, the executive proposed that Red Top be permitted to enter the taxi cab market in Arlington County. The existing cab company opposed the proposal. We approved the proposal and the existing cab company sued. The attorney representing Red Top was a friend of mine and I told him that the opposing cab company had not come before the commission and therefore had not exhausted its administrative remedies before going to court. The Virginia Supreme Court threw out the case. I think we did the right thing.

One of my favorite civic activities was at the Calvary Foundation. It was 1970; I was listening to political speeches at the church when the Reverend Via tapped me on the shoulder and said, "Woody, we want you back here." That was the beginning of long pro bono service. It was also the beginning of the Calvary Foundation.

The brainchild of another lawyer, General Faw, the foundation was incorporated by him, an employee of the IRS, and me. The first board of directors elected me the first president. It was an experience.

The IRS did not approve tax exemption for the foundation. It continued to ask for more information. Roy Hale, a neighbor and fellow board member said, "Woody, let's go down to IRS and see what's holding this up."

We got an appointment and went downtown, expecting to meet with distinguished-looking gentlemen with grey hair; instead we were greeted by two young men with long hair. They said the initial ten-thousand dollar donation by Colonel Lynn should have been made out to the church first, then to the foundation.

I said, "That is exactly the way it was done."

The IRS official said, "You'll have your approval in 30 days."

I also served as counsel for fifteen years. Sometimes I had to be firm with members who made proposals with which that I did not agree. At the end of fifteen years, the board established a policy with which I did not agree and I resigned.

Another board member, a retired lieutenant colonel, said that he admired me for resigning. I didn't think the foundation was going to grow financially. However, it is my understanding that the permanent endowment is now close to five hundred thousand dollars before the stock market tanked. Scholarships for deserving students are granted from the interest earnings.

My political career was rather short. I ran for committee man from Virginia Highlands where our first house was located. I was associated with Leo Urbanski who, along with his mother, was entrenched in local Democrat politics. I ran against a local man who had served Virginia Highlands for a long time. I won hands down.

While serving on the committee, I was asked to run for delegate to the historic Virginia Assembly. As a Democrat, running for delegate victory was all but guaranteed. I would have loved to serve. But my solo law practice had taken off. I would have had to be away from my wife and three children, and my practice. My corporate clients would not have stood for long absences, so I turned it down. I felt my service at the American Law Division and as an attorney and legal digester qualified me to be a good legislator. Reluctantly I declined.

Another of my civic endeavors was as president of the Nellie Custis Parent-Teachers' Association. This was the elementary school my daughter Elaine attended. In 1960, there was no kindergarten, kindergarten room, or multi-purpose room there. I had resigned from my very secure attorney job at the American Law Division to enter solo law practice in Arlington. When I was selected as president of the Parent-Teachers' Association, I considered it an honor. With my wife at home, three children, and a mortgage to pay, I still helped with the children and house work as much as I could. I could not take on another civic job.

Now you might say that President of the PTA is not much of a job—I beg your pardon—it is one helluva job.

Now get this—here I am, embarking on an unknown path, with one major civic responsibility, when the civic association calls me and asks me to be president of the Jefferson Civic League. The Jefferson Civic League was instrumental in getting the county to purchase the land for the Fort Scott Park. Thousands of people have enjoyed this Park. See picture. Enough is enough. I said no.

The previous year I had been chairperson of the committee to obtain the funds for the addition for Nellie Custis.

As PTA President, the association was in the midst of trying to secure $350,000 from the county to fund such improvements. To complete the project, we also needed to exercise the right of eminent domain and take two houses. I wasn't aware of this until later, when a member of the Arlington Bar told me he had been contacted by one of the owners who planned to sue me. No suit was ever filed. These are the risks of civic work. Pro bono work. Of course, he had no case.

We supported Leo Urbanski for the county board. He assisted greatly in raising the money. He had been a student at Nellie Custis. Members of the PTA and I attended several board meetings. Though it was not always easy and it was sometimes contentious, we got the funding for the kindergarten, and the additions were built. Today, Nellie Custis is used for the handicapped and for elections.

Our first son, Jonathan, went to Mrs. King's kindergarten. Our second son, Bill went to Calvary Methodist Church kindergarten, which was run by Mrs. Ford.

I went to kindergarten in Greenville, Michigan, at the Pearl Street School. My mother was president of the PTA.

Chapter XIII

Family

While on the subject of elementary schooling, let me talk a little bit about my daughter Elaine. She was chosen from Custis to go to Oakridge for an advanced talented class. Two children were chosen from each elementary school in Arlington. The authorities said she did not have perfect grades, but her best friend did. Elaine was chosen because of her emotional stability and maturity.

The class was learning about the law. For one exercise, Elaine was chosen to be the judge. The teacher asked me to lecture the students about law. I accepted. Those kids asked the same questions that a mature audience might have asked, like, "How can you defend a client you know is guilty?" Of course, the Constitutional Right to Counsel.

Elaine was a good student and I will never understand why she wasn't accepted at the University of Virginia. She spent her freshman year at the University of Colorado. She worked summers at Yellowstone Park. From there she went on to graduate from the College of William and Mary.

Graduate studies included Duke University Divinity School, and Elaine graduated in the top ten of a very large class. Then she came to the fork in the road that my high school classmate Fred Meijers talks about. She was interviewed by the bishop. He wanted to send her to a rural area. She didn't want to go—the Bishop said she was not dedicated. Back home she was down in the dumps, and told me she had an expensive education she couldn't use. I told her, "Elaine, you will use that Divinity degree all through your life."

It was prophetic.

While in New Hampshire to see the bishop, Elaine applied for a job at Dartmouth Hospital. She became a medical technician at Dartmouth.

While taking prerequisite science courses for Duke's physician assistant program, she landed a job that would use all of her education. Her employers were impressed, and because of her Divinity degree, gave her the psychiatric job, claiming that they could use her services at half the price of a doctor. So the Divinity degree at Duke was an expensive education, which she could use after all!

My son Bill went to Virginia Commonwealth University for one semester. One day he called home and said, "Dad, you are wasting your money—I want to get out into the real world." He had a hammer in his hand when he was two years old. His junior year in high school, he spent the summer at the farm built a pretty room on the second floor of the barn. He also helped Leroy Compton build a foundation under the barn. That room served as a place for us to stay on weekends while paying for the land. It had a window, a fan, and a hot plate. After we built the cedar house, Ray Smelser, who helped Rick Matthews build a wood fence around the house, said "It—the room—served its purpose." Bill has a very successful general contractors business.

The house has a large farm kitchen, a bathroom, a well that goes down 250 feet in solid rock with twenty gallons of pressure per minute, air conditioning, electric heat, a neat New England wood-burning stove, a porch, two bedrooms enlarged at Bill's suggestion; all the comforts of home.

Jon, our oldest son, is employed by the postal service. He has the best retirement plan in the country. He went to college in Colorado for one year and got very good grades, especially in accounting. He married Jackie before going off to school—we financed her last year of high school.

Unfortunately, Jon and Jackie separated. However, he returned to marry Kathy. Jon is a very good worker. He helps me with yardwork at home and on the farm, now that I am retired.

John married a pretty girl Kathy in 1976. She is a very good sales lady in the furniture business; however, she really is focused on interior design. She received a BA degree from Marymount University in interior design in May of 2008. She graduated summa cum laude. She attained this degree by taking one or two subjects at a time while working full time. It took her ten years to get her degree. Now *that* is perseverance.

She designed the new decor in the farmhouse. Her white horse, Dakota is at the farm. When the man who sold her the horse brought Dakota down to the farm, he looked around at the Shenandoah National Park and said, this horse is going to think he is in horse heaven. The park borders the back of the 128-acre farm.

Bill married a girl in 1984 named Anne. They have one child, Jonathan Neal Walker. He is very good at using the computer and internet. He has recently taken more of an interest in the farm, helping with taking care of the horses and splitting wood. He assisted my son Bill in planting ninety-five black walnut seedlings among the stumps of our recent harvesting of black walnuts. There is a picture of him standing on black walnut logs. Anne is now an assistant to a veterinarian here in Arlington. She has a very tender heart for animals and is in the right line of work. Bill says his house is like a zoo.

They, Billy and Jonathan Neal go down to the farm every weekend. At that time, Bill visits his mother, Janet in the nursing home. And she, Anne, takes care of the house and helps keeping the stables clean. She recently had a bout with cancer, but it had been cured.

Chapter XIV

Close Calls

I have already related some other close call. When we first bought the farm, there was a bag of corn cobs in the woodshed. I went into the woodshed to take the corn cobs out and, lo and behold, out came a swarm of yellow jackets. I swung my hat around my head to keep them away from my face and ran out and fortunately was able to jump into the car. I had a thin undershirt on and five of the yellow jackets had stung me through that thin shirt. I felt like I had been electrocuted.

The yellow jackets attacked the windshield and windows of the car but couldn't get in. I turned on the air conditioner and applied some vaseline that I had in the car. The vaseline seemed to help and I survived.

I also had a close call on the farm involving rattlesnakes—twice. During the first one I was looking for a stray steer in the brush. From my peripheral vision, I saw something coming at me from the left side—I made a quick jump to the right—he was rattling, striking. I did not attempt to go looking for him in the brush. Walking out into the clean field (we called it Gyspy's Field), I could see blood coming through my white shirt. My thought was, *He got me.* My Boy Scout training saved me – *Do not run, do not panic; walk to the gate and road.*

There I met Billy Elkins, a neighbor. I asked Billy, "Would you drive me to the hospital? I think I have been poisoned." At the hospital, the ER doctor said, "Mr. Walker, your quick jump to the right saved you. The snake bit you but did not poison you."

The blind man, Wiley, in the snack box at the courthouse said, "Woody, the Lord was with you." My colleague next to my law office, Harry Lee Thomas— an excellent lawyer—said, "Woody, now what kind of a story is that."

I said, "All right you doubting Thomas, let me show the two fang marks in my left arm." Harry Lee was convinced.

The next run-in with a rattlesnake was with Marie, a young girl, niece of my daughter-in-law, Anne. Marie was just taken with horses, and of course we had two horses at the farm. On this particular weekend there were a large number of people at the farm. The horses were nowhere in sight. Marie wanted to see the horses. I said, "Okay, Marie, let us get the halters and see if we can find them." I told Marie, "Now you stay behind me—I do not think we will run into a rattlesnake, but you never know." We walked all the way around the farm, in the woods. At this point, Marie became very excited. I asked, "Marie, what is the matter?" She pointed close to where I was standing, saying, "snake, snake." I said, "Marie, you get behind me."

I did not have a gun, a stick—anything with which to fight the snake. I walked right by that snake. He could have nailed me in the leg. I picked up a flat rock and hit him on the head, rolling him over. He had huge rattlers as big as an Eastern Diamondback's. I was told I got too close to this deadly snake, for he could jump and hit you in the throat, but I was so concerned for the safety of this little girl that I threw caution to the wind.

Jonathon Neal said, "He felt sorry for the snake."

I said, "Do not. If he had nailed me or Marie, especially Marie, he could have killed or at least made the one of us who got bitten extremely sick."

Now, we are not prejudiced against all snakes. We had a black snake living in the farm that kept the rat population down for years. We called him "Blackie." I tell newcomers to leave that snake alone and to not harm him.

While on the subject of close calls, recently (in 2006), I was coming home from the farm in my Chevrolet pickup on Route 55, where it goes down to Green Hills. At the top of the hill the speed limit changes to 55 from 45. Now, it should be lowered because you pick up speed going down the hill. At the bottom of the hill a very nice young lady was getting ready to make a left-hand turn into Green Hills. At the time I saw her I could see I could not stop in time. You have to think fast in these situations. As all of you drivers know, of course, the thing to do is to swing to the left to avoid hitting her; however, there was another car in that lane.

I made a quick decision to avoid hitting her in the rear and just missed her—I could see the people in the other car. I thought, *Here we go in a head-on collision.*

I could not believe it but I squeezed between both of them, barely scraping her Mitsubishi. I asked her, "What were you doing sitting at the bottom of the hill?"

She said, "I live in Green Hills."

I said, "You will be paid." I had no damage to speak of. I said, "There is no need to call the police. I will take care of it."

She insisted. I said, "All right."

A veteran Virginia State Police officer from Winchester answered the call. His name was Wilkinson. He said there would be no charges. He had us exchange information. He said there is not even a card going to be put in this case. As I recall, the repair to her car cost only twelve hundred dollars, paid by my insurance company. This close call was certainly as close as I have ever come to meeting my maker, including my World War II experiences. Changing the speed limit going down that hill from 45 to 55 miles per hour did not make sense. I was going to write the Virginia DMV about it. However, they had just recently changed it to 45 MPH.

We have had a number of close calls in regard to copperhead snakes on the farm, but they are not quite as dangerous as the eastern diamondback rattler. I was at the back of the large field walking toward the farm downhill, admiring the beautiful sunset. Fortunately I had my single-barrel twelve gauge shotgun with me. Copperheads do not warn you—they are quiet.

For some reason, I looked down. If I hadn't my next step would have been on him, a huge, old copperhead. I stepped back and fired. The shot did not kill him. I fired again, this time blasting off his head. Of course, a shotgun's shot reverberates in the mountains. My neighbor Larivee came over and asked, "What is all this shooting about?" I picked up a stick and held up the dead copperhead and said, "This is what all the shooting is about."

Janet and I were in the horse stables. She was cleaning out the manger when she let out a scream that would awaken the dead. She pointed to the beam next to the manger. There was a small copperhead. Fortunately it did not bite her.

I trust that you have found this book interesting.